JOSEPH CONRAD

Carl D. Bennett

D0170985

A Frederick Ungar Book
CONTINUUM · NEW YORK

1991
The Continuum Publishing Company
370 Lexington Avenue, New York, NY 10017

Copyright © 1991 by Carl D. Bennett

Printed in the United States of America

Library of Congress Cataloging-in-Publication Data

Bennett, Carl D.
    Joseph Conrad / Carl D. Bennett.
        p.   cm.—(Literature and life. British writers)
    "A Frederick Ungar book."
    Includes bibliographical references and index.
    ISBN 0-8264-0531-2 (cloth)
    1. Conrad, Joseph, 1857–1924.   2. Novelists, English—20th
century—Biography.   I. Title.   II. Series.
PR6005.O4Z5613   1991
823'.912—dc20
[B]   91-8713
                                                                  CIP

JOSEPH CONRAD

LITERATURE AND LIFE: BRITISH WRITERS

Select list of titles in this series:

W. H. AUDEN	*Wendell Stacy Johnson*
JANE AUSTEN	*June Dwyer*
THE BRONTËS	*Bettina L. Knapp*
ANTHONY BURGESS	*Samuel Coale*
NOEL COWARD	*Robert F. Kiernan*
ARTHUR CONAN DOYLE	*Don Richard Cox*
T. S. ELIOT	*Burton Raffel*
FORD MADOX FORD	*Sondra J. Stang*
E. M. FORSTER	*Claude J. Summers*
FRIVOLITY UNBOUND: SIX MASTERS OF THE CAMP NOVEL	*Robert F. Kiernan*
ROBERT GRAVES	*Katherine Snipes*
GRAHAM GREENE	*Richard Kelly*
ALDOUS HUXLEY	*Guinevera A. Nance*
CHRISTOPHER ISHERWOOD	*Claude J. Summers*
JAMES JOYCE	*Bernard Benstock*
KATHERINE MANSFIELD	*Rhoda B. Nathan*
CHRISTOPHER MARLOWE	*Gerald Pinciss*
JOHN MASEFIELD	*June Dwyer*
W. SOMERSET MAUGHAM	*Archie K. Loss*
JOHN MILTON	*Gerald J. Schiffhorst*
V. S. NAIPAUL	*Richard Kelly*
BARBARA PYM	*Robert Emmet Long*
JEAN RHYS	*Arnold E. Davidson*
SIR WALTER SCOTT	*Edward Wagenknecht*
SHAKESPEARE'S COMEDIES	*Jack A. Vaughn*
SHAKESPEARE'S HISTORIES	*George J. Becker*
SHAKESPEARE'S TRAGEDIES	*Phyliss Rackin*
MURIEL SPARK	*Velma Bourgeois Richmond*
TOM STOPPARD	*Felicia Hardison Londré*
J. R. R. TOLKIEN	*Katharyn W. Crabbe*
EVELYN WAUGH	*Katharyn W. Crabbe*
H. G. WELLS	*Brian Murray*
WILLIAM BUTLER YEATS (PLAYS)	*Anthony Bradley*
THE POETRY OF WILLIAM BUTLER YEATS	*William H. O'Donnell*

Complete list of titles in the series available from the publisher on request.

For Margaret

Contents

Preface

Another book about Joseph Conrad?

I confess to a modest hope that this treatment of the man and his work will appeal to those who, like Conrad, have thought about the mystery of human motivation and action in a complex world of cross purposes and unforeseen consequences.

The ideas generated here are the result of many years of association first with my mentors and then with my own students, to whom I owe a deep debt for countless unremembered exchanges in and out of class.

Of course I have gained much from the contributions of Conrad scholars and from conversations with my colleagues at St. Andrews College.

A first draft of a portion of this material was printed as "A Choice of Nightmares" in the *St. Andrews Review*.

For my wife and daughters I express special gratitude for their patience and unswerving support.

C. D. B.
February 1991

Chronology

1857   On December 3, at or near Berdyczów (Berdichev), Poland, Józef Teodor Konrad Korzeniowski is born, the only child of Apollo Korzeniowski and Ewa Bobrowska.

1861   Apollo is arrested for revolutionary activities and the following year he and his wife are deported into Russia. Their small child suffers with them the severe hardships of exile and illness.

1865   Conrad's mother dies in Chernigov, Russia. His father is allowed to change his place of exile to Lwów, in Austrian Poland.

1869   Father and son move to Kraków, where Apollo dies. The orphaned child becomes the ward of his mother's brother Tadeusz Bobrowski.

1874–   Conrad, still a teenager, goes to Marseilles, where
77   he enters the French merchant marine. During these years he completes a number of voyages to the Caribbean area, and in 1877 seems to have engaged in some gunrunning escapades, probably on behalf of the Spanish pretender Don Carlos.

1878   In February 1878 Conrad is presumed to have shot himself in the chest, an incident that for years was disguised as a duel. On April 24, having been rescued from his financial difficulties by Uncle Tadeusz, Conrad sails as an ordinary seaman on the British steamer *Mavis*. On June 10, he lands at Lowestoft, his first visit to England. During his sixteen years with the British merchant service he will voyage to many of the ports of Asia and the South Pacific.

1884   He sails on the *Narcissus* from Bombay to Dunkirk.

1886   Conrad becomes a British citizen, and shortly thereafter receives his certificate as a master mariner.

1888   Conrad assumes his only sea command, as captain of the barque *Otago,* and sails from Bangkok.

1889   Conrad resigns his command in Adelaide and returns to London. The czarist government releases him from the status of a Russian subject. Conrad begins his first novel, *Almayer's Folly.*

1890   In Brussels, he secures an appointment as captain of an African river steamer. After four months in the Belgian Congo, having contracted malaria and dysentery, he returns to Europe.

1891   Recuperating slowly, he takes temporary employment in a London warehouse and possibly as a translator. In November he sails as first mate on the clipper *Torrens;* in the next two years he will make two voyages to Australia.

1893   Conrad travels to the Ukraine for a last visit with Tadeusz Bobrowski.

1894   His appointment as first officer of the *Adowa* ends when its voyage to Canada is canceled, and Conrad's sea career is at an end.

1895   *Almayer's Folly* is published under the name of Joseph Conrad.

1896   Conrad marries Jessie Emmeline George. *An Outcast of the Islands* is published. Conrad abandons a novel, *The Sisters,* never completed. He begins another work, "The Rescuer," which will evolve into *The Rescue,* a novel not finished for over twenty years.

1897   *The Nigger of the "Narcissus"* is published.

1898   The Conrads' first son, Borys, is born. *Tales of Unrest* is published. "Youth," the first of Conrad's stories to present Charlie Marlow as narrator/participant, is printed in *Blackwood's Magazine*.

1899   "Heart of Darkness" appears in *Blackwood's*.

1900   *Lord Jim* is published.

1901   *The Inheritors*, written with Ford Madox Ford, is published.

1902   *Youth, A Narrative, and Two Other Stories*, including "Heart of Darkness," is published

1903   *Typhoon, and Other Stories* is published. *Romance*, written with Ford, is published.

1904   Jessie Conrad suffers a serious knee injury, which leaves her permanently lame. *Nostromo* is published.

1905   Conrad receives £500 from the Royal Bounty Fund.

1906   *The Mirror of the Sea* is published. The Conrads' second son, John, is born.

1907   *The Secret Agent* is published.

1908   *A Set of Six* is published.

1910   "The Secret Sharer" appears in *Harper's Magazine*.

1911   Conrad is the recipient of an annual Civil List Pension of £100. *Under Western Eyes* is published.

1912   *A Personal Record* (first printed as *Some Reminiscences*) is published, as is *'Twixt Land and Sea*, including "The Secret Sharer."

1913   *Chance* is published.

1914   The Conrads travel with friends to Poland. War breaks out, and with some difficulty they make their way back to England.

1915   Son Borys enlists at seventeen, is commissioned, and is soon at the front. Conrad himself joins coast patrols and once flies over the North Sea. *Within the Tides* and *Victory* are published.

1917   *The Shadow-Line* is published.

1918   Borys is gassed and shell-shocked a month before the armistice.

1919   A dramatization of *Victory* is performed at the Globe Theatre, and Conrad starts to work on a dramatization of *The Secret Agent*. He sells film rights to his works. *The Arrow of Gold* is published.

1920   Conrad completes a series of author's notes for a collected edition of his works. *The Rescue* is published. Conrad begins work on a Napoleonic novel, *Suspense,* left unfinished.

1921   The Conrads travel to Corsica. *Notes on Life and Letters* is published.

1922   Conrad's dramatization of *The Secret Agent* is performed in London.

1923   Conrad spends a month in New York. *The Rover* is published.

1924   Conrad declines a knighthood. He dies suddenly August 7, and is buried in Canterbury.

1925   *Tales of Hearsay* is posthumously published; the unfinished *Suspense* is published, as is *The Congo Diary*.

1926   *Last Essays* is published.

1928   *The Sisters,* an early fragment, is published.

1

Biography

Józef Teodor Konrad Korzeniowski was born December 3, 1857, at or near Berdyczów (Berdichev), Poland.[1] He was the only child of Apollo Korzeniowski (coat of arms Nałęcz) and Ewa (or Evelina) Bobrowska, also of the landed gentry. Both families were identified with Polish aspirations for freedom from czarist Russian rule. Apollo, a poet and translator as well as patriot and revolutionary, was accepted with some reluctance by the Bobrowskis. He and Ewa were married May 8, 1856.

In October 1861 Apollo was arrested for revolutionary activities in Warsaw, and the following May he and Ewa, both charged with conspiracy, were deported into Russia, first to the frozen quagmire of Vologda, then to Chernigov. Their small child suffered with them the severe hardships of exile. In these circumstances Apollo managed to complete translations of Dickens, Hugo, and Shakespeare, though his son was frail, and his wife's health steadily declined.

In the third year of their ordeal Conrad's mother died. And at last, early in 1868, the father, broken in health, was allowed to change his place of exile to Lwów, in Austrian Poland. In the summer of 1868 the boy himself entered a period of fragile health, and frequently was seriously ill. Apollo, along with his writing, tutored little Konradek until failing strength obliged him to give the boy's education over to others. But Conrad's enforced isolation and his father's example cultivated in him a taste for literature. He read Apollo's translations of Shakespeare, Victor Hugo, Alfred de Vigny, and Dickens; and he early discovered Cervantes and Alain-René Lesage, Cooper and Frederick Marryat, and Polish writers of epic and romance; he reveled in books of history, travel, and exploration.

In later years he would learn from Stendhal, Balzac, Flaubert, Maupassant, Zola, Anatole France, and Turgenev. He was influenced by writers as different as Dostoyevsky and Melville, although he expressed distaste for the American's "portentous mysticism" and he rejected Dostoyevsky as "too Russian for me."[2] His mature thought was influenced by Schopenhauer and Asian religions, notably Buddhism.

Apollo Korzeniowski and his son moved to Kraków in February 1869, and three months later Conrad's father died. At first the orphaned child came under the guardianship of Apollo's close friend Stefan Buszczyński, who placed Conrad in a pension for boys. Then in 1870 he was taken by his maternal grandmother, Teofila Bobrowska, whose concern for Conrad's welfare had brought her to be near her grandson. She remained in Kraków with the boy for the next three years, until May 1873. At this time Conrad became the ward of Ewa's brother Tadeusz Bobrowski, who all the while had been providing the funds for the boy's upkeep. This stern but affectionate uncle remained Conrad's austere mentor and benefactor until Bobrowski's death in 1894.

Conrad's education during these years was unsystematic and intermittent. He later claimed to have attended Saint Anne's Gymnasium in Kraków, but records do not confirm this. It is known that his Uncle Tadeusz employed as Conrad's private tutor a young medical student named Adam Marek Pulman. Pulman accompanied Conrad to Krynica in the summer of 1870, and in May 1873 they went together to Switzerland, and then visited Munich, Vienna, and northern Italy. In August 1873 Bobrowski sent his nephew to Lwów, where he was placed, along with other boys orphaned by the 1863 insurrection, in a boardinghouse operated by a cousin, Antoni Syroczyński. Except for an occasional excursion with Pulman, Conrad remained in Lwów for a year, but in September 1874 Bobrowski removed his nephew from school, and thus was ended Conrad's formal education.

During this time Conrad, against a family tradition of worshiping the holy land of Poland, had begun to press for permission to go to sea. In October 1874, shortly before his seventeenth birthday, Conrad traveled to Marseilles, alone but with letters of introduction from his uncle and the assurance of a generous allowance from his patrimony. His associations in the French port city included the Royalist family of Jean-Baptiste Delestang, whose members were deeply involved in efforts to restore Don Carlos de Borbón to the throne of Spain. With the aid of the Delestangs and others, Conrad quickly acquired sailing skills and confirmed his love of the sea. His first deep-water voyage was experienced as a passenger on the *Mont Blanc*, on a trip that took him to Martinique and back, between December 1874 and May 1875. Within a month he sailed for the West Indies again, this time as an apprentice seaman. He was in Marseilles again by the year's end.

In July 1876 Conrad sailed as a steward on the barque *Saint-Antoine*. The first mate was Dominic Cervoni, who served later as a model for more than one fictional character. Besides St. Pierre, Martinique, the ship visited ports in Colombia and Venezuela, areas that provided Conrad for the setting of *Nostromo*. After further stops in the Caribbean, the *Saint-Antoine* returned to Marseilles in February 1877.

During these years, Conrad seems to have engaged in some illicit escapades, once thought to be gunrunning activity on behalf of Don Carlos, but perhaps instead some smuggling ventures connected with South American revolution. By Conrad's own account, he did sail with Dominic Cervoni, whom he depicted as an Odyssean model of heroism and ingenuity. And, possibly, during these same years, he formed a romantic attachment with a young lady of Carlist sympathies. What is more certain is that sometime early in 1878, because of debts and other personal difficulties, Conrad shot himself in the chest, an incident that was for years disguised as a duel. All his Marseilles experiences are effectively obscured in *The Mirror of the Sea* and other memoirs, in the novels *The Arrow of Gold* and *The Rover*, and in a fictional fragment, *The Sisters*. Such were Conrad's mythmaking proclivities that it is imprudent to trust any of his autobiographical statements.

In April 1878 Conrad sailed from Marseilles as an ordinary

seaman on the British steamer *Mavis*, bound for Constanti-
nople with a load of coal. On June 18 the ship docked at
Lowestoft, and for the first time he set foot on English soil.

Within a few weeks he had signed as an able-bodied seaman
on a coal schooner, *Skimmer of the Sea*, and he made three
round trips from Lowestoft to Newcastle. Conrad later wrote
that it was in that craft he "began to learn English."[3] Since
the pay was so low he left the schooner in September and
went off to London, where he managed to negotiate a berth
on a wool clipper, *The Duke of Sutherland*, bound for Australia. The ship left England in October on its more than three
months' voyage around the Cape of Good Hope, arriving in
Sydney the last day of January 1879. During the long delay
waiting for a return cargo, Conrad was night watchman on
the moored vessel. The ship returned to England, presumably
by way of Cape Horn, arriving in London the middle of
October 1879.

Conrad's next voyage, on the steamer *Europa*, took him
to the Mediterranean. He returned to London the end of
January 1880, and then followed some months of unem-
ployment. A curious episode, puzzling to Conrad's chroni-
clers, involves a letter Conrad wrote his uncle in August,
reporting an alleged accident on the clipper *Annie Frost* (or
Anna Frost), together with the loss of belongings and a subsequent hospital stay. Conrad's report may well have been a
tale to inspire sympathy in a time of financial embarrassment,
aggravated by loss in unwise speculation of some of the
money his uncle had sent him. There seems to be no question
that Conrad, in such matters as the application for a second
mate's certificate, was prone to deceive by exaggerating or
even inventing supporting facts. Incidentally, he did pass the
examination in May 1880 and was awarded his certificate,
much to the delight of his Uncle Tadeusz.

After months of idleness, Conrad finally obtained an assignment as third mate on the *Loch Etive*, an iron clipper
that left London in August 1880 bound for Australia. The
voyage, which took approximately a hundred days each way,
ended back in London the following April.

Then, on September 19, 1881, Conrad signed as second

mate on the ill-fated barque *Palestine*. After a series of troubles, the unseaworthy vessel was loaded with coal and set out for Bangkok a year later, on September 17, 1882. The cargo caught fire and the ship was abandoned in the Java Sea. This disaster is recalled in *Youth*, and the subsequent court of inquiry in Singapore is reflected in *Lord Jim*. Conrad returned to England as a passenger on a steamer. After a brief holiday with his Uncle Tadeusz, in 1883, he again went to sea, this time on the clipper *Riversdale*, which sailed from London to Madras, arriving in April 1884. There Conrad was dismissed by the captain, whose refusal to give him a completely positive reference would later cause a delay in Conrad's application for a first mate's certificate.

Six weeks later Conrad sailed from Bombay as second mate on an iron sailing ship, the *Narcissus*, arriving at Dunkirk the middle of October. This and other voyages provided the store of incident and characters that are fictionalized in his sea stories.

In December 1884, after a second examination, he received his certificate as chief officer, more than four years after attaining his paper as second mate. Preferring sailing vessels to steamships, he had to wait till April 1885 for an assignment, still as second mate, on the clipper *Tilkhurst*. This voyage, lasting over a year, took him from Hull to Singapore and Calcutta.

During his stay in Asian ports Conrad wrote several letters to Joseph Spiridion Kliszczewski, son of a Polish émigré who went to England after one of the many failed insurrections against Russian rule. Aside from being the earliest examples of his writing in English, the letters are important for two reasons. They reveal Conrad's consuming interest in politics, both on the Continent and in his newly adopted land— "When speaking, writing or thinking in English the word Home always means for me the hospitable shores of Great Britain." His conservative instincts are finding expression: he wonders which British statesman can stop "the rush of social-democratic ideas," for "socialism must inevitably end in Caesarism." Second, he displays in the letters what would become a persistent habit of casting about for ways to enter into business partnerships and other moneymaking ventures. Here he contemplates raising capital for the purchase of a whaling vessel![4]

But his Uncle Tadeusz was urging Conrad to more practical measures—to seek British citizenship and his certificate as master mariner. Conrad returned to London in June 1886 and the next month tried and failed his first examination. In November he was successful and received his master's certificate. Meanwhile, in August, he had become a naturalized British subject. Both of these achievements were pleasing to his uncle, but Bobrowski continued to press Conrad to divest himself of dual citizenship in order to avoid any liability to czarist conscription, a release he was not able to secure from Russian authorities until March 1889.

Conrad's career as a ship's officer did not measurably improve. Early in January 1887, after less than a week aboard, he left the frigate *Falconhurst* at Penarth, and in Amsterdam the next month he signed as first mate on an iron barque, the *Highland Forest,* captained by John McWhir and bound for Semarang in Java. Injured at sea, Conrad was eventually hospitalized briefly in Singapore. In August he signed as mate on an island trader, the *Vidar.* Conrad made at least four trips on this vessel that, though it was owned by an Arab trader, sailed under the British flag and was captained by an Englishman. He traveled up the Berau River (formerly the Pantai) in Borneo, an important locale for Conrad's Malay novels and tales, and the area of operations for the merchant-adventurer William Lingard and his protégé Olmeijer, both originals of Conrad characters.

In January 1888, while considering a return to London and a try at the business side of maritime life, Conrad obtained his only sea command, as captain of the small iron barque *Otago,* made possible by the death of the former captain. This experience of the loneliness and responsibility of "first command" was re-created in *The Shadow-Line* and provided a psychological dimension to "The Secret Sharer." In some fifteen months Conrad took the *Otago,* laden variously with teakwood, fertilizer, and grain, from Bangkok to Singapore, the Malay archipelago, Australia, and Mauritius. During this time the young captain tentatively entered into the social life of the colonies' European residents; and in Port Louis, Mauritius, even became involved in brief romantic attachments. Some of these island experiences were later assimilated into short stories. Conrad was remembered at this time as being something of a dandy. His dress and manners earned him the ironic title of "the Russian Count."[5]

In the spring of 1889, Conrad abruptly resigned his command, and sailed as passenger on a German steamer from Adelaide to Southampton. Sometime that autumn he began his first novel, *Almayer's Folly*, and a long uncertain transition from sea life to professional writing was under way. During this period he was associated in some kind of work relationship with one or more shipping companies in London, and he sought contacts with various nautical firms in hopes of securing a command or other position abroad.

In November 1889 Conrad interviewed Albert Thys, of the Société Anonyme Belge pour le Commerce du Haut-Congo, and in his effort to obtain an appointment went to Brussels the following February and enlisted the aid of a distant cousin and his wife. The cousin died suddenly, but this visit was the beginning of a long friendship with the widow, "Aunt" Marguerite Poradowska, who was herself a published author. Before embarking on his assignment in Africa, Conrad traveled to Poland, left sixteen years before, and spent two months with his Uncle Tadeusz on the Bobrowski estate at Kazimierówka. His stay was not altogether pleasant, for in the society of young Polish patriots, Conrad was made to feel uneasy about abandoning his fatherland. It is interesting to note that during these months Conrad was conversing daily in Polish, writing letters in French, and thinking in English as he worked on the manuscript of *Almayer's Folly*.

In May 1890 he sailed from Bordeaux for the Belgian Congo, where he was slated to take command of a small river steamer, the *Florida*. It turned out that the vessel was wrecked and instead he was assigned to the stern-wheeler *Roi des Belges*, manned by a young Danish captain named Koch, a Belgian mechanic, and twenty or so black crewmen. Others who made the month-long trip up the Congo included the

company manager, Camille Delcommune, and three of his
agents. Conrad's correspondence at the time has left evidence
that mutual antipathy quickly developed between Conrad and
his fellow Europeans. Also the journey up the Congo, including a grueling overland march to Leopoldville (now Kin-
shasha) as well as the river passage from there to Stanley
Falls, enabled him to observe the colonial depredations
against the African continent and its native inhabitants. Conrad's experiences, first partially recorded in a diary still extant,
and in letters written to Marguerite Poradowska and others,
were eventually to take fictional shape in "Heart of Darkness," a powerfully symbolic projection of his vision of European colonialism with its confusion, stupidity, cruelty,
greed, and duplicity, all masquerading as philanthropy. At
the end of his life Conrad was still looking back at the African
exploitation by Leopold II and other imperialists as "the vilest
scramble for loot that ever disfigured the history of human
conscience and geographical exploration."[6]

The company agent at Stanley Falls, Georges Antoine Klein,
was taken aboard ill and died on the return downstream. He
would become Kurtz in "Heart of Darkness." Conrad himself
fell victim to dysentery and fever and, after a harrowing six
weeks' journey to the coast, returned to London and entered
a hospital. He was to suffer the effects of this illness for the
remainder of his life. Conrad later remarked that the only
baggage he brought back with him from Africa was a pair
of stories, "An Outpost of Progress" and "Heart of Darkness." But he had been hauling with him the early chapters
of *Almayer's Folly*, and he managed to preserve the manuscript from disaster.

For months after his return from Africa, Conrad suffered
intermittent attacks of gout, neuralgia, malaria, and depres-
sion. At length, with the encouragement of his Uncle Tadeusz,
he went to Champel-les-Bains, a spa near Geneva, where the
water cure mitigated his symptoms.

In spite of continuing physical and mental distress, he secured work in the warehouse of a London shipping firm, and
he took on occasional chores of translating business letters

from Slavonic languages into English, and he possibly translated some Polish short stories as well.

In November 1891 he obtained a berth as first mate on the
passenger clipper *Torrens,* bound for Adelaide. In Australia
Conrad learned from letters that a cousin, Stanislaw Bobrowski, was imprisoned in the same dungeon where Apollo
Korzeniowski had been held thirty years before. The *Torrens*
returned to London in September. On a second voyage to
Australia, beginning in October 1892, a Cambridge student,
William Henry Jacques, read and approved the unfinished
manuscript of Conrad's first novel. On the return from Adelaide to London the spring of 1893, Conrad met two youthful
passengers, Edward Lancelot "Ted" Sanderson and John
Galsworthy, both of whom became lifelong friends.[7]

In August 1893 Conrad left the *Torrens* and paid a final
visit to his Uncle Tadeusz in Poland. At year's end he signed
on as first officer of the *Adowa,* but in January 1894 the
ship's voyage was canceled at Rouen. Although Conrad
would be trying for another berth as late as 1898, his sea
career was at an end.

But Conrad had been working for five years on his manuscript, and in April 1894 he completed *Almayer's Folly.*
Meanwhile Tadeusz Bobrowski had died suddenly in February, and his nephew was staggered by this loss of moral
and financial support. Conrad's letters to Mme. Poradowska
during 1894 reveal the intense nervousness with which he
awaited word from a publisher. In August he went again to
Champel for the water cure, and while there appears to have
begun writing what turned out to be his second novel, *An
Outcast of the Islands.* Conrad returned to London in September and in October received word that his first book had
been accepted by T. Fisher Unwin. The novel, dedicated to
his uncle, was published in April 1895.[8]

From the start, although it would be years before his writing achieved any popular or financial success, Conrad received encouragement from reviewers, including H. G. Wells.
One of the readers for Unwin was Edward Garnett. The
friendship of this younger man proved of incalculable benefit

to the lonely and insecure Conrad, for Garnett continued to support and advise him throughout his career.

Conrad's life from May 1895 to the spring of 1896 was complicated by relationships with at least three women, Marguerite Poradowska, with whom he continued an intimate correspondence, and two young ladies barely half his age—he was then thirty-eight. One was Mlle. Emilie Briquel, whose family he met at Champel. Their flirtation seemed for a time to be developing into a real courtship, and Emilie even began a French translation of *Almayer's Folly*. But Conrad had been introduced the previous fall to Miss Jessie Emmeline George; and, although he continued to write to Emilie, his friendship with Jessie progressed into the fall of 1895, during the time he was completing work on *An Outcast of the Islands*. In December he suddenly proposed and she accepted, and they were married on March 24, 1896.

Much speculation has centered on Conrad's decision to choose a spouse with so different a cultural background. When they met, Jessie was working in London as a typist. Her family included her widowed mother and eight other children, and although Conrad insisted to friends that he was "not marrying the whole family," there would be times when their existence complicated an already precarious financial or emotional situation. To Garnett, who was among those who wondered if the projected marriage was a wise one, Conrad wrote (just hours before the wedding!): "There remains nothing but the surrender to one's impulses, the fidelity to passing emotions which is perhaps a nearer approach to truth than any other philosophy of life. . . . I would rather grasp the solid satisfaction of my wrong-headedness and shake my fist at the idiotic mystery of Heaven."[9]

Following a civil ceremony in London the couple went for their honeymoon to Ile-Grande, in Brittany, a stay that extended to September 1896. A short story, "The Idiots," written during this period, is a tale about a mother of several idiots who kills her husband to prevent conception of another child—a work that, as Zdzisław Najder remarks, "was to provide great fun for all Conrad's future psychoanalytic critics."[10]

In the fall of 1895 Conrad had begun an abortive novel, *The Sisters;* it was abandoned about the time of his marriage in March 1896, and the fragment was not published in his lifetime. In the letter to Garnett the day before his marriage, Conrad announced a new "sea-story," to be called "The Rescuer: A Tale of Shallow Waters." This novel, not completed for more than twenty years, was finally published in 1920 as *The Rescue: A Romance of the Shallows.*

Conrad and his wife returned to England in the fall of 1896, and soon settled in a semidetached house in Stanford-le-Hope, Essex, near the Thames estuary; and the following spring they rented Ivy Walls, a larger and more comfortable property in sight of the Thames. A near neighbor was G. F. W. Hope, a longtime friend with whom he enjoyed frequent sailing excursions in the English Channel. During these months Conrad completed several stories, including "Karain," "The Return," "An Outpost of Progress," and "The Lagoon." He was also working on *The Nigger of the "Narcissus,"* which was serialized and published late in 1897.

August of 1897 was especially significant, for Conrad then wrote for this book the preface containing the celebrated comments on his moral and aesthetic aims.[11] And in the same month Conrad received from R. B. Cunninghame Graham a letter praising "An Outpost of Progress" for its sharp criticism of colonialism. Conrad responded and there developed a lifelong friendship, and one of the strangest, for Cunninghame Graham was a well-known figure whose radical career while a member of Parliament in the eighties included imprisonment for illegal leftist activity, and he had participated as well in the Congress of the Second International in Paris. Conrad, in spite of his antisocialist views, apparently was drawn to Graham by shared aristocratic tastes and, at a deeper level perhaps, by a common skepticism concerning the efficacy of human institutions. The long and fruitful relationship with Cunninghame Graham called forth some of Conrad's best expressions of his private views.

Other friendships were being formed by Conrad at this time. In the fall of 1897 he began a warm and personal association with Stephen Crane, the young American author

of a critically acclaimed novel, *The Red Badge of Courage.*
That friendship was tragically brief, for Crane's short and
action-packed life would end within three years. Another new
acquaintance, also a transplanted American, was Henry
James, an established literary figure with an international
reputation. Conrad had taken the initiative in October 1896
by sending James a copy of *An Outcast of the Islands,* cov-
ering his hesitation with an effusive note inscribed on the
flyleaf. James responded in February 1897 by sending Conrad
a copy of *The Spoils of Poynton.* And in December 1897
Conrad sent off to his "Cher Maître" a copy of *The Nigger
of the "Narcissus."* Thus began a professional relationship
that through the years remained distant though mutually re-
spectful. Even when they became neighbors in Kent, theirs
was not an intimate friendship.

On January 15, 1898, the Conrads' first son, Borys, was
born. Conrad's ambivalent feelings regarding the event may
be inferred from his correspondence with close friends. When
the child was a year old, he confided to Helen Sanderson that
he would have preferred a daughter; Borys, he added, "is an
accomplished and fascinating barbarian full of charming
wiles and of pitiless selfishness. It is not his innocence but his
unconsciousness that makes him pathetic—besides making
him just bearable."[12]

During these months Conrad was struggling with his writing—he had taken up "The Rescuer" again—and at the same
time he was desperately borrowing money from friends. His
situation was relieved somewhat when his first volume of
stories, *Tales of Unrest,* published in March 1898, was
awarded a prize of fifty guineas. Finding "The Rescuer" in-
tractable, he now tried a new approach. He began to write
the stories that present Charlie Marlow as narrator/partici-
pant. The first to be completed was "Youth," published in
Blackwood's Magazine in June 1898. "Heart of Darkness"
began to run in *Blackwood's* in February 1899. "Tuan Jim:
A Sketch," possibly the earliest of the pieces containing Marlow, gradually evolved into *Lord Jim,* which began serialization in October 1899 and was published the following
October.

Meanwhile in the fall of 1898, after a futile trip to Glasgow in a final effort to obtain a sea command, Conrad had moved his family to Pent Farm, in Kent. The red brick cottage was rented from a young writer named Hueffer (later Ford Madox Ford). In the same area lived Stephen and Cora Crane, the H. G. Wellses, and Henry James. So it was that Conrad was able to develop profitable associations in a widening circle of literary friends. His visitors here included old friends like Galsworthy and Garnett and Graham and new acquaintances, among them George Gissing, W. H. Hudson, George Bernard Shaw, and the artist William Rothenstein.

While living at Pent Farm, Conrad entered on a period of collaboration with Ford that produced two novels: *The Inheritors* (1901) and *Romance* (1903).[13] Their joint effort, while ineffectual, did at last confirm Conrad as a professional writer. His finances, chronically in a precarious condition, improved slightly as Edmund Gosse, William Rothenstein, Henry James, and others secured for Conrad various royal grants; and John Galsworthy, among many others, was constant in his offers of loans and other support. But the Conrads during the next decade were rarely free of financial exigencies, often precipitated or aggravated by the serious illness of one or both of the boys (John Alexander Conrad was born August 2, 1906), by Jessie Conrad's prolonged difficulties with a knee injury suffered early in 1904, or by Conrad's own frequent sieges with gout or neurosis. His literary agent, James Brand Pinker, who for more than twenty years after 1900 was the family's mainstay, often rescued the desperate Conrad with generous advances.

During the years Conrad was collaborating with Ford, he wrote some short pieces, including two of his best: "Typhoon" and "Amy Foster." Another tale, "The End of the Tether," was published along with "Heart of Darkness" in *Youth, a Narrative; and Two Other Stories,* in 1902. At the suggestion of Sidney Colvin, library director at the British Museum, Conrad rewrote his story "To-morrow" as a one-act play, *One Day More,* which, though it pleased critics such as Max Beerbohm and the formidable Shaw himself, lasted only five performances. In this as in other projects he had the

assistance of Ford. During the same time Conrad was beginning what he thought would be another short work, but
which over two rough years evolved into a masterpiece, *Nostromo*. A collection, *Typhoon, and Other Stories*, published
early in 1903, gained public esteem for its author, but *Nostromo*, published in London and New York by Harper, in
1904, received disappointing reviews.

Conrad's letters written while he was struggling with *Nostromo* comprise a litany of anxiety and self-accusation. To
Galsworthy, for example, he wrote:

> To work in the conditions which are, I suppose, the outcome of
> my character mainly, is belittling—it is demoralising. I fight against
> demoralisation of which fight I bear the brunt and my friends bear
> the rest. . . . I feel myself—strangely growing into a sort of outcast.
> A mental and moral outcast. I hear of nothing—I think of nothing—
> I reflect upon nothing—I cut myself off—and with all that I can
> just only keep going or rather keep on lagging from one wretched
> story to another—and always deeper in the mire.[14]

Yet to Galsworthy, and to other young writers as well, Conrad was unstinting with helpful suggestions regarding style
and structure. To Ford's wife Elsie he gave advice on translating Maupassant, and to Ford himself he offered support
in numerous ways—in 1908 Conrad helped substantially in
the founding of the *English Review*, which Ford edited brilliantly for a brief period.

Conrad's relationship with Ford was unquestionably sym-
biotic. During their earlier collaboration Ford hit on the strategy of taking Conrad's dictation of "memories and
impressions," which were shaped into a collection called *The
Mirror of the Sea*, published in 1906. And during the time
of Ford's connection with the *English Review*, Conrad was
persuaded to contribute some essays of crucial autobiographical interest. They took their place in a collection, *Some Reminiscences*, published in 1912 and soon retitled *A Personal
Record*.

Following the first of many operations on Jessie's knee, the
Conrads left for Capri in January 1905. There Conrad met
Norman Douglas, and they were visited by John and Ada

Galsworthy. But from the start the trip with the disabled Jessie was a progressive disaster. Unexpected expenses, assorted illnesses, and Conrad's frustration over his writing drove the family back to England. They did not fare much better at home. By the end of the year Jessie was in her second pregnancy, lame and becoming obese, and showing signs of a heart ailment and nervous prostration. At the same time Borys was hospitalized with scarlet fever, and Conrad himself suffered a severe attack of gout.

Nevertheless Conrad succeeded by year's end in writing a couple of stories, both of them dealing with anarchism. And early in 1906, while staying at a health resort in Montpellier, he began a third story dealing with anarchists. This was "Verloc," which evolved soon into *The Secret Agent*. In December 1906, soon after the birth of John Alexander, the family went again to Montpellier, where they spent a number of months and, in the spring of 1907, they went to Geneva. Dangerous illnesses of the children blighted this stay on the Continent, but Conrad had managed to finish *The Secret Agent* late in 1906, and it was published by Algernon Methuen in September 1907. Again the reviews were disappointing.

In September 1907 a fierce argument with Ford over Conrad's considerable debt for back rent owed on Pent Farm led to another move, this time to the Someries, a house in Bedfordshire. (This was the first Conrad home to boast indoor plumbing.)

In these months Conrad was working intermittently on *Chance,* a novel that had been in his mind for three or four years, one providing a fictional reprise of Marlow. But the work stalled, as it had done on the still unfinished *Rescue.* In December 1907 he began "Razumov" as a short story that would grow into a full-length novel, *Under Western Eyes.* The following August he gathered stories from assorted periodicals and published them as *A Set of Six.* But Conrad was being tormented by criticism that his work would be more welcome if first written in Polish and then translated into English! And he was sinking ever deeper into debt: his royalties for the year totaled less than five pounds, by his own account, and he owed over £2000 to Pinker and to various close friends. (By 1910, his accumulated debts rose to £2700, a figure equal to nearly $100,000 in 1991 dollars.)

Conrad completed *Under Western Eyes* around the end of 1909, but events were building toward emotional catastrophe. Early in 1909 he and his family had moved to Aldington, where they occupied four rooms over a butcher shop with a view of the slaughterhouse from the bedroom windows. A quarrel with Ford over some of the autobiographical material scheduled for the *New Review,* an angry confrontation with Ford's estranged wife Elsie, and a raging row with his faithful agent, Pinker, all prodded the fatigued author into a severe breakdown that lasted for several months. A personal disappointment came in 1910 when his son Borys, then twelve, failed to pass examinations that would have qualified him for a university education. Because of the boy's nearsightedness, Conrad was able to secure only a limited acceptance for Borys aboard the Royal Navy training ship *Worcester.*

"The Secret Sharer," written during the final weeks Conrad was struggling with *Under Western Eyes,* was the only significant piece to appear during 1910. One of his finest short stories, it was printed in the August and September issues of *Harper's Magazine.*

In spite of continuing serious illness Conrad managed to revise *Under Western Eyes* while it was running serially in the *English Review* and the *North American Review,* and its appearance in book form in the fall of 1911 marked the publication of Conrad's first novel in four years. Reviewers generally liked the book, and his spirits were boosted when the novelist Arnold Bennett sent him an enthusiastic letter of praise. Conrad was also making a fresh beginning on *Chance;* and for his projected collection of essays he wrote "A Familiar Preface," a splendid update of his ethical and aesthetic credo.

Conrad's health was improving, and the family had been moved into a much more appealing residence, Capel House in Orlestone. The rise in his fortunes was further signaled by an award of a Civil List pension. Still another source of income was assured for succeeding years when a wealthy American lawyer, John Quinn, began buying Conrad's manuscripts. Further, Conrad was making new friends of a younger generation, among them Richard Curle, author in 1914 of the first book on Conrad, and André Gide, who visited him and undertook to translate *Typhoon* into French. Later, Gide supervised the translation of other works, and he became a powerful advocate of Conrad to Continental readers.

In January 1912 Harper published Conrad's essay collection as *Some Reminiscences* (it was later retitled *A Personal Record*). And the same month the long awaited *Chance* began serialization in the *New York Herald*. As usual Conrad worked feverishly on revisions as the installments were appearing. For publication the following October, he was preparing *'Twixt Land and Sea,* a collection of stories that included "The Secret Sharer," "A Smile of Fortune," and "Freya of the Seven Isles." The reviewers' response to *'Twixt Land and Sea* was strong, and for the first time the public reception promised to match the critical respect that Conrad's work had earned from the days of *Nigger of the "Narcissus"* and *Lord Jim*. Conrad was particularly pleased when Edith Wharton praised "The Secret Sharer" and suggested to him that it be translated into French.

In this peak period of productivity during his fifty-fifth year, Conrad had also begun working on a new novel, "Berg" or "Dollars," which he would eventually turn into *Victory*. In the spring of 1913 Frank Nelson Doubleday, the American publisher, visited Conrad; and soon Doubleday's young editor Alfred A. Knopf was making plans for the publication of *Chance*. No doubt with Conrad's approval, Knopf shrewdly undertook to promote the book by means of critical blurbs collected from popular contemporaries, and when it appeared in January 1914 it became a near best-seller on both sides of the Atlantic.

During this busy time Conrad continued to widen his circle of admirers, among them the French poet and statesman St.-John Perse and the American author Ellen Glasgow. The Cambridge scholar Bertrand Russell, already an established mathematician and philosopher, visited him more than once. Their correspondence reflects mutual esteem, expressed touchingly on Russell's part when in 1921 he named his son for the novelist. Conrad was not so lucky with his revered master and near neighbor Henry James. One day in 1913, for example, the Conrads received an invitation to visit James and drove to Rye only to be informed that he was "out." And the next year James wrote a long article for the *Times Literary Supplement* in which he mixed praise of Conrad with some sharp strictures on *Chance*. The writer who for Conrad had been a model of novelistic art criticized him for espousing "the way to do a thing that shall make it undergo most doing"—in other words, for subordinating content to excessive technique.[15] James's words, while a fair judgment on the novel's involuted structure, were grievous to Conrad, who privately acknowledged (after James's death) "that this was the *only* time a criticism affected me painfully."[16]

But the public was at last hooked on Conrad. *Lord Jim* was reissued in a large edition and sold well. Richard Curle's book, *Joseph Conrad, a Study,* though not well received, at least kept the author's name in readers' minds. Conrad was readying *Victory* for serialization and, with finances greatly improved, he agreed in the summer of 1914 to take his family and travel with Mr. and Mrs. Józef Retinger to Poland.

In Kraków he visited the university where his father's papers were preserved. Then, while at the country estate of a friend, Conrad learned that World War I had begun. He and his family took temporary refuge with Aniela Zagórska in Zakopane, but were soon caught in the chaos of mobilization and barely escaped internment for the duration. They arrived safely in England after weeks of hardship and anxiety. Conrad's son Borys obtained a commission and was at the front by October 1915. Conrad's time during the war years was filled with worry for the safety of Borys (who was gassed and shell-shocked a month before the armistice in 1918) as well as concern for friends who were facing death in France (Edward Thomas, a young poet friend, was killed in action); and he was often distracted by the precarious condition of Jessie, who was periodically threatened with amputation of her disabled leg. But he did join a few coast patrols against enemy submarines and once flew over the North Sea.

And he stayed busy and reasonably productive. *Victory*

was published in 1915, and also a collection of stories, *Within the Tides*. *The Shadow-Line*, a short narrative Conrad claimed was "not a story really but exact autobiography,"[17] was serialized in 1916 and published in 1917. His new wartime acquaintances included the novelist Hugh Walpole, whom Conrad later called "the most intimate of my younger friends."[18] A book by Walpole and another by an American, Wilson Follett, both published in 1916, were signs that Conrad was attaining classic status. The same year a bust of Conrad was completed by Jo Davidson. Meanwhile he and his publishers were planning a collected edition of his major works. In June 1918 he completed the manuscript for *The Arrow of Gold*, based on his early Marseilles experiences but presenting as heroine a young woman modeled in part on Jane Anderson, an American journalist whose frequent stays with the Conrads during the war years distracted the entire household.

In July he turned to a final encounter with *The Rescue*, which had tormented him for all the years since he started it in 1896. By January 1919, in spite of more surgery on Jessie's knee and bouts of flu all around, Conrad had both *The Rescue* and *The Arrow of Gold* running serially and was wondering which to publish first. The real consideration, ironically, was Conrad's desire to impress the Nobel Prize committee that year. As it turned out, *The Arrow of Gold* appeared in 1919 and *The Rescue* was published in 1920, and Conrad was passed over for the only honor he had openly coveted.

But Conrad at least was freed from further financial stress, for in June 1919 he had sold the movie rights to his works for more than £3000. He was also continuing his tentative experiments with the theater. He began work on his own stage adaptation of *The Secret Agent* in October 1919, soon after the Conrads moved to their last home, Oswalds, in Bishopsbourne, near Canterbury. The next year he even tried his hand at writing a film scenario based on an early story, "Gaspar Ruiz." The script, now lost, was never filmed.

And Conrad was wrestling again with *Suspense*, a novel begun in 1912 and set in the Napoleonic era. He wrote his agent Pinker on May 11, 1920: "I am tackling in good earnest today the Elba Novel and mean to continue from day to day if the heavens fall."[19]

Early in 1921 Conrad published *Notes on Life and Letters,* which contained, besides some affectionate if not always accurate reminiscences about his sea life, a selection of essays on some of his favorite writers: Turgenev, Maupassant, Alphonse Daudet, Anatole France, Stephen Crane, and Henry James. The book is also interesting for calling forth a comment by E. M. Forster, who expressed his judgment that Conrad "is misty in the middle as well as at the edges, that the secret casket of his genius contains a vapour rather than a jewel. . . . No creed, in fact. Only opinions, and the right to throw them overboard when facts make them look absurd."[20]

Forster's review no doubt stung Conrad, but not all reviewers in these years were reserved or unfriendly. Still to be counted on were faithful associates like Garnett, who continued to write intelligent and supportive critiques; and new voices were added, as when Katherine Mansfield praised *The Rescue.* Even Virginia Woolf, a Bloomsbury associate of Forster who wrote an anonymous review attacking the same novel, nevertheless expressed her admiration for the man and his gift.[21]

In January 1921, with son John enrolled in a boarding school at Tonbridge, Conrad set out with Jessie for Corsica; they were accompanied at first by Borys, who showed them some battle sites in France. At Rouen they were joined by Georges Jean-Aubry, a young member of André Gide's literary circle, who accompanied them as far as Lyons. Jean-Aubry was associated with Gide in the French translations of Conrad's works, and ultimately became Conrad's first biographer. From Marseilles Conrad and Jessie went to Ajaccio, where he researched the Napoleonic background of the novel he was dictating to his secretary, Lillian Hallowes. He enjoyed conversations with the Pinkers and other visitors on Corsica, and was particularly stimulated by some debates with a young admirer of Dostoyevsky and Freudian psychology.

The Conrads returned to England in April in time to succor

Borys, who had lost his job in the failure of a business firm. At this time Conrad, in a reversal of his lifetime pattern, was subsidizing others, including Jessie's mother and a Polish cousin, Karola Zagórska. He and Jessie also continued to entertain the many guests who visited Oswalds.

In May 1921 a Polish playwright, Bruno Winawer, sent Conrad the text of a play, *The Book of Job*, with a request for help in finding a translator and a London producer. Conrad found the wry comedy amusing and himself went to work on the translation and even tried to persuade an acquaintance to stage the piece. This activity was related to Conrad's continuing interest in producing stage and cinematic versions of his own works. He was deeply immersed in the dramatizations of *Victory* (in March 1919) and *The Secret Agent* (in November 1922)—he even wrote the script himself for the latter play, but stayed away from all ten performances. Conrad's career in the theater exhibits a close parallel with that of Henry James, whose serious experiments with the stage were disastrous.[22]

In October 1921, frustrated by the stalled *Suspense*, Conrad began another story of the Napoleonic era, *The Rover*. As was so often the case he expected the tale to be a short one, but it grew into a full-length novel that he completed in record time, by June of the following year. Meanwhile, with Borys's financial problems added to his own, Conrad was considering a move to southern France where he could live inexpensively and escape British taxes. His abiding love for France was no doubt strengthened by his old ties with Gide and Jean-Aubry and his new acquaintance with the poet Paul Valéry and the composer Maurice Ravel. Certainly it was his strained finances that led Conrad in December 1922 to accept Doubleday's invitation to visit America, and the following spring he spent six weeks in New York. There he met another distinguished Polish expatriate, the pianist-composer Paderewski. Conrad, during his stay at Doubleday's home on Long Island, was shielded from the curious (F. Scott Fitzgerald and Ring Lardner were driven off the lawn one evening when they tried to attract attention), but he was not spared a peculiar American ordeal, the press conference. More satisfactory than facing the crowd of journalists was an evening as guest in a Park Avenue home where, in a thick accent that surprised some of his listeners, he read passages from *Victory* to a select audience of two hundred. He wrote Jessie: "After the applause from the audience, which stood up when I appeared, had ceased I had a moment of positive anguish. . . . There was a most attentive silence, some laughs and at the end, when I read the chapter of Lena's death, audible snuffling."[23]

After a brief tour of New England, Conrad returned home, where he was dismayed to learn that Borys had been secretly married before the visit to America. In the fall he took a final trip to France to arrange for his younger son, John, to spend a year with friends of Gide. His final novel, *The Rover,* was published in December 1923.

In January 1924 his grandson Philip was born. In March, Conrad agreed to sit for a bust by Jacob Epstein, an American sculptor of Polish extraction. In May he received an offer of a knighthood, which he declined, as he had rejected all offers of honorary degrees. In June he was honored at a luncheon in London at the Polish legation. On the first weekend of August, Richard Curle visited Oswalds and Conrad talked about the unfinished novel, *Suspense.* In good spirits, he told Curle that his mind was clearer than in months, and added, "I shall soon get hold of my work again."[24]

But on the morning of Sunday, August 3, Conrad died of a heart attack. Four days later he was buried in Canterbury.

2

Introduction: Awareness beyond Ability

In *A Personal Record* (1912), his most important autobiographical work, Joseph Conrad wrote: "The ethical view of the universe involves us at last in so many cruel and absurd contradictions, where the last vestiges of faith, hope, charity, and even of reason itself, seem ready to perish, that I have come to suspect that the aim of creation cannot be ethical at all."[1]

Yet no modern author has wrestled more valiantly than Conrad with the ethical dimension of human existence. He was a man whose naturally sensitive temperament was shaped by a childhood made wretched and gloomy by the early death of his parents, and by a general atmosphere of resentful humiliation in his native Poland, then oppressed by czarist Russia, and when he grew up and left home, by a lifelong sense of inadequacy—fostered in him by stern if affectionate relatives, by his disappointments and frustrations in his sea life and in his career as a writer—all things by which, as G. Jean-Aubry said, "unconsciously he was being trained in a secret and inflexible fidelity to ideals dissociated from hope."[2]

In his personal life and in his relationships with others, Conrad could never escape his strong sense of moral responsibility. To Helen Watson, Conrad wrote (June 27, 1897) concerning the man she was to marry: "He is not the man to abandon the ethical position in which his sensitive conscience has placed him for his fight with life."[3] Obviously Conrad was reading the characterization of his friend out of himself. In his fiction as well as his own affairs the matter of ethics was crucial. Writing to his literary agent, J. B. Pinker, in 1907, Conrad reported some research on Napoleon at Elba, done for the novel *Suspense*. He told Pinker: "All I want now is to discover the moral pivot—and the thing will be done."[4] Ten years later he iterated his artistic creed in a letter to Sidney Colvin:

All my concern has been with the "ideal" value of things, events, and people. That and nothing else. . . . En vérité c'est les valeurs idéales des faits gestes humains qui se sont imposés à mon activité artistique. Whatever narrative and dramatic gifts I may have are always, instinctively, used with that object—to get at, to bring forth *les valeurs idéales*.[5]

In his persistent inquiry into the ethical aspects of human nature, Conrad was never forgetful of the fact that men and women are best understood not as mere thinkers but rather as actors. Human actions proceed from a mystifying variety of deliberative and random elements. This mysterious combination of purpose and impulse results in activity that can be called conscious in varying degree. Conrad's quest for meaning is bound up in this concept of humans acting. To the extent that they are conscious, their actions may be equated with choosing, with valuing. To the extent that humans choose or evaluate, they are capable of feeling responsible during the act, or after the event when responsibility may modulate to guilt. A genuine sense of responsibility or guilt is accompanied by suffering. This suffering is due, in part, to a sense of opportunities lost, of values destroyed or not allowed to come into being. Marlow, in *Lord Jim*, is made by Conrad to say that Jim was "aware" with "an intensity that made him touching, just as a man's more intense life makes his death more touching than the death of a tree." The title character of *Lord Jim* (1900) is a natural point of reference for the construction of a "typology" of Conrad's ethical agents, for Jim illustrates in his complex personality each of three levels of consciousness in the human beings who inhabit Conrad's fiction. As a basis for this typology, I have devised a formula, *awareness beyond ability*, meant to imply an individual's awareness of the inability to control means and ends—an awareness of the treachery of freedom, or one's sense of freedom, which is associated with all definitions of tragedy.

If this concept of tragic awareness beyond ability is applied to Conrad's fiction generally, his characters fall fairly into three categories: First, there are those who are merely "aware," which for Conrad will prove to be falsely aware. That is, abstracting from the world of their sensations, they have constructed an ideal view of reality that is illusory. Jim, for example, at the outset of his career suffers a momentary humiliation because he is not "ready" to play the hero in a training emergency. The captain's sympathetic "Better luck next time" and Jim's imperfect awareness of himself enable him to make a quick recovery of his self-image, and "he exulted with fresh certitude in his avidity for adventure, and in a sense of many-sided courage."

Then, second, there are those characters who are "able" without being particularly self-conscious of their powers. Typically, they are "unconscious" like Singleton in *The Nigger of the "Narcissus"* (1897). Life is ordered for these so that their resources prove satisfyingly adequate for whatever they are called upon to do. Stein, in *Lord Jim* (1900), was in Marlow's view one of these lucky ones: "This man possessed an intrepidity of spirit and a physical courage that could have been called reckless had it not been like a natural function of the body—say good digestion, for instance—completely unconscious of itself." Jim, too, had his moments of unreflecting and satisfying achievement, especially in the early years of his Malayan period, when as Lord Jim he "regulated so many things in Patusan."

Finally, there are those who are fully aware beyond their ability. Jim, for much of the time at least (he is admittedly a special case), was aware in this sense. His awareness of responsible involvement, of complicity if not guilt, implies in Jim a conviction of personal freedom that can be tragically thwarted by deficiencies within as well as without. That he fought against recognizing this responsible freedom does not remove him from consideration here. This sense of responsibility is present in all truly conscious men and women, Conrad knew. The intensely aware person is the one with a high degree of consciousness. When consciousness becomes aware of obligation, one has conscience, the key to a person's character, the appraisal of one's own activity.

For Conrad, who went from Polish to English by way of French, the word *conscience* embraces all that *consciousness* means, not merely the morally judging aspect.[6] In the same way, it seems to me, *awareness* for Conrad means more than the apprehension of "moral truths." It also means more than the perception of physical data. I do not believe that Conrad was concerned to deny the veridical aspect of sensory perception. One is "falsely aware" when one is falsely aware of oneself in the world. That is to say, one's awareness of self in relation to the world is incomplete. For Conrad this becomes crucial when the character's incomplete or defective awareness proceeds from or is betrayed by a failure to acknowledge moral limitations. Complete awareness of the (whole) self would imply conscious acknowledgment of personal moral deficiency in a morally ambiguous world. This awareness of a flawed self in a flawed universe constitutes tragic awareness.

There is no doubt that Conrad was skeptical about the real extent of human freedom. In *Nostromo* (1904), he wrote: "Action is consolatory. It is the enemy of thought and the friend of flattering illusions. Only in the conduct of our action can we find the sense of mastery over the Fates." Over and over Conrad's fiction illustrates the ironic truth about an individual who when he or she is most conscious of freedom may be observed by fellow mortals to be a prisoner of circumstances, not merely those natural and social conditions that "stand around" one, but also those forces of life that operate within one and through one to fulfill purposes, or to bring consequences beyond one's calculation or expectation, or even outside the limits of one's hopes and fears. But, along with these demonstrations that we are the frequent victims of the illusion of freedom, Conrad sets forth some men and women whose exquisite sense of moral responsibility is rooted in the conviction that they do possess a meaningful degree of freedom. It is this sense of freedom that adds poignancy to the tragic conflict within human beings when they are faced with irreconcilable choices joined with the necessity to act.[7] Tragic awareness, for Conrad, comes—it may be before, during, or after the act—whenever the character realizes personal inadequacy, an inability under the shadow of a heavy moral obligation to control either the intention or the consequence of the action.

In the chapters that follow, my attention will be directed toward works of major significance, particularly those that illustrate Conrad's concern with ethical dilemmas. In all cases, my chief aim will be to present Conrad's understanding of the basic levels of human awareness. I do not expect to apply my typology rigidly—this was implied in my choice of Lord Jim as a paradigm of three ways of being aware. I do not think that Conrad or any responsible critic of the novelist has supposed that the living creatures of his art are reducible to *types*. My belief is that this kind of analysis, moderately handled, is a fair one and I hope it will be a fruitful one. I hope also that this inquiry into the nature of Conrad's ethical and aesthetic vision will result in the framing, at least by implication, of a meaningful theory of tragedy.

3

Ethical Agents Who Are Falsely Aware: *Almayer's Folly* and *An Outcast of the Islands*

The two novels to be discussed in this chapter were published in the period when Conrad was moving from sea life to fiction writing. Altogether he spent sixteen years in the British merchant service, voyaging to many ports of Asia and the South Pacific. But as early as 1889 he began a novel while on shipboard, and although he was trying to obtain another sea assignment as late as 1898, he moved doggedly toward his destiny as one of the principal writers of the late nineteenth and early twentieth centuries.

Almayer's Folly (1895) and *An Outcast of the Islands* (1896) are sometimes dismissed from critical consideration, But the two Malayan novels may be read as a double earnest of Conrad's story-telling abilities. Into tropical settings depicted with impressionist and symbolic power, Conrad gathered Englishmen, Dutchmen, Arabs, and Malays all snarled in an intricacy of personal and political impulses.[1] And he worked with psychological certainty to develop themes of self-deception and betrayal that would absorb him throughout his artistic life.

From these two earliest novels can be drawn a pair of Conrad's specimens who display a false sense of awareness: Kaspar Almayer, who inhabits both Malay books, and Peter Willems, who joins him in the second novel. Both Almayer and Willems turn out to be ethical agents who abstract from their world an illusory view of reality. In terms of their illusions and of their own sensations these characters may be excruciatingly aware, but their very real pain and humiliation is—for the reader—effectively neutralized by the ironic perception Conrad brings to bear on his material. Genuinely tragic suffering is negated by the sense of the ridiculous or despicable or pathetic Conrad arouses in his readers. Both men fall short of a sense of moral responsibity beyond their powers. Neither man achieves tragic awareness beyond ability.

Almayer of *Almayer's Folly*

Kaspar Almayer, in the view of the omniscient author, was a "grey-headed and foolish dreamer." Years before he had left his home in Holland "ready to conquer the world, never doubting that he would." As the protégé-partner of an English trader named Tom Lingard,[2] Almayer had invested his hopes in a remote and sluggish trading post in Borneo. Into the bargain, he had taken on at Lingard's urging a Malay girl for a wife. Conrad reports that Almayer "was gifted with a strong and active imagination." In his fancy, he had projected a life of wealth and ease as heir someday to old Lingard, and as for the native wife, "He had a vague idea of shutting her up somewhere, anywhere, out of his gorgeous future."

Things do not work out however. Almayer now is "a man busy contemplating the wreckage of his past in the dawn of new hopes." The new hopes are focused on his half-breed daughter, Nina, and this in spite of the fact that she has grown up with a marked partiality for her mother's people. Convinced it is the only way to insure his dream of splendid wealth, Almayer betrays to some natives the passage up the river to Lingard's mines. But success eludes him again. When the Dutch authorities charge him with disloyalty in selling gunpowder to the natives, Almayer defends himself violently: "What have you ever done to make me loyal? . . . When I asked for protection I was met with threats and contempt, and had Arab slander thrown in my face. I! a white man!"

At the first intimation of new failure Almayer harangues Nina, ranting about this false sense of betrayal. His anger dies and he feels ashamed at his outburst,

yet relieved to think that now he had laid clear before his daughter
the inner meaning of his life. He thought so in perfect good faith,
deceived by the emotional estimate of his motives, unable to see
the crookedness of his ways, the unreality of his aims, the futility
of his regrets.

Conrad pointedly suggests Almayer's deepening self-delusion in scenes that occasionally approach the surreal. These
hallucinatory episodes depict a progressive loss of contact
with reality as first his wife leaves him and then his daughter
runs away with Dain Maroola.

When Nina and Dain have departed, Almayer gets down
on his hands and knees and, creeping along the sand, carefully erases all traces of his daughter's footsteps. Later, in
an effort to destroy every vestige of Nina's existence, he
burns his quarters and moves to the unfinished house,
"Almayer's Folly." There he ends his days in an opium stupor,
a final comment by Conrad on Almayer's estrangement from
reality.

Critics, assaying Conrad's first novel, have variously isolated textual evidence of sentimentality, pathos, even tragedy;
I feel that the distinctive element is irony. Certainly this is in
keeping with the author's intention, as he confirmed in *A
Personal Record*. There he describes the original Olmeijer as
a man whose conduct was governed by "incredible assump-
tions, which rendered his logic impenetrable to any reasonable person," and to him he addresses an ironic apostrophe:
"You were always an unlucky man, Almayer. Nothing was
ever quite worthy of you. What made you so real to me was
that you held this lofty theory with some force of conviction
and with an admirable consistency" (pp. 76, 88). Thus Conrad
commented on his first specimen of a human being who is
excruciatingly but falsely aware of himself and of his relation
to the world.

Willems of *An Outcast of the Islands*

Conrad's second novel, *An Outcast of the Islands*, goes back
some fifteen years to the same Malay locale as that of *Al-*

mayer's Folly. Many of the same characters are present, including Lingard and his protégé Almayer and Nina, now just a five-year-old child. In this book the moral interest centers on another of Lingard's protégés, Peter Willems, who like Almayer is dream-obsessed to the last moment of his life. *An Outcast of the Islands* is a more complicated work than the first novel. And its greater length allows more attention to contextual considerations like colonial rivalries and native intrigues. Conrad's profound understanding of human society is displayed in the way he concretizes native life with its own special forms of treachery and rapaciousness and at the same time provides case studies of the disastrous consequence of imperialist intrusions into tribal communities.[3] The focus remains, however, on Peter Willems, another example of a consciousness that is falsely aware of itself and of the reality that confines it. And Conrad presents him with an icy contempt that rules out any sympathy for his sufferings.

The first view of Willems is characteristic. On the way home from his job as confidential clerk of Hudig & Co., he has stopped for drinks and a game of billiards, "slightly dizzy with the cocktails and with the intoxication of his own glory." And, exulting, he reviews his exploits—"the quiet deal in opium; the illegal traffic in gunpowder; the great affair of smuggled firearms, the difficult business of the Rajah of Goak." The omniscient author comments that Willems

disapproved of the elementary dishonesty that dips the hand in the cash-box, but one could evade the laws and push the principles of trade to their furthest consequences. Some call that cheating. Those are the fools, the weak, the contemptible. The wise, the strong, the respected, have no scruples. Where there are scruples there can be no power.

So Conrad describes his Schopenhauerian/Nietzchean parody. And so he iterates his motif of a burlesque providence, doubling the God-figure Lingard who "created" Almayer in the first novel. The power-loving Willems feeds and clothes all his wife's half-caste relations: "He kept them singing his praises in the midst of their laziness, of their dirt, of their immense and hopeless squalor: . . . It is a fine thing to be a providence, and to be told so on every day of one's life."

Conrad does not detail the crime of Hudig's confidential clerk, reporting simply that "almost before he was well aware of it he was off the path of his peculiar honesty." Hudig finds out about the embezzlement and fires him. Tom Lingard intervenes and arranges for the disgraced Willems to join Almayer at his trading post in Sambir. As might be expected, the two protégés of Lingard are uneasy in the company of each other. Willems, in particular, suffers: "It was only himself that seemed to be left outside the scheme of creation."

Then Willems meets Aïssa, daughter of the royal fugitive Omar. Conrad gives lyric expression to their encounter, but Willems's romance with Aïssa is not to be a redemptive experience. He wins her without joy and contrary to the image of his self-constructed dream. Conrad reports that Willems "had a sudden moment of lucidity—of that cruel lucidity that comes once in life to the most benighted. He seemed to see what went on within him, and was horrified at the strange sight."

But this is not the full illumination of horror that Conrad reserved for Kurtz in "Heart of Darkness." Willems's awareness, no matter how exquisitely torturous, is flawed by self-delusion. Willems is horrified because he is

a white man whose worst fault till then had been a little want of judgment and too much confidence in the rectitude of his kind! . . . He seemed to be surrendering to a wild creature the unstained purity of his life, of his race, of his civilization.

Willems's surrender to Aïssa is made more galling by his knowledge that he is being used by her people in the complicated politics of Malay, Arab, and European. He "measured dismally the depth of his degradation. He—a white man, the admired of white men, was held by those miserable savages whose tool he was about to become." Conrad comments on Willems's suffering:

He was not, of course, able to discern clearly the causes of his misery; but there are none so ignorant as not to know suffering, none so simple as not to feel and suffer from the shock of warring impulses. The ignorant must feel and suffer from their complexity as well as the wisest; but to them the pain of struggle and defeat appears strange, mysterious, remediable, and unjust.

It is this sense of injustice that destroys Willems's fidelity. First he lies to Aïssa. Then he betrays his benefactor, Tom Lingard, by piloting Abdullah up Lingard's secret river. He is punished by the special justice of Lingard, who decides to hide his "mistake." In spite of his pleas to be permitted to return to civilization, Willems is left with Aïssa in the jungle where, significantly, the world of tropical nature plays its part in sapping the manhood of Willems.

Critics since Thomas Moser have tended to dismiss Conrad's treatment of sexual matters as deficient, and some critics have even employed psychoanalytic strategies to explain the author's supposed discomfort in dealing with sex.[4] Be that as it may, and considering the Victorian restraints regarding explicit scenes, Conrad's handling of Willems's luckless passion for Aïssa seems adequate. He writes that Willems "took her in his arms and waited for the transport, for the madness, for the sensations remembered and lost; and while she sobbed gently on his breast he held her and felt cold, sick, tired, exasperated with his failure—and ended by cursing himself."

Defeated by impotence, Willems realizes that he is trapped in a perverted paradise, companioned by an impossible Eve, robbed of the consolation of passion as well as his freedom of movement. With the passage of time his subjectivity is exacerbated by fever and exhaustion. Conrad says, "Like most men, he had carried solemnly within his breast the whole universe, and the approaching end of all things in the destruction of his own personality filled him with paralyzing awe." In a remarkable image prescient of Freudian symbolism, Willems is pictured in the fetal posture, motionless under a great jungle tree.

To this spot comes Mrs. Willems, directed there by the vengefulness of Almayer. Conrad depicts "this meeting of lawful love and sincere joy" with ghastly irony. Willems is full of dread and suspicion of his wife, but he recognizes that she offers a means to escape Aïssa and the jungle. But when Aïssa returns and sights the landing party, she misjudges the situation, arms herself with Willems's revolver and rushes to his aid. She soon understands the real situation and, outraged, orders him to leave. Willems, daring not to leave unarmed, determines to take the weapon from her. In a remarkably surrealist scene Conrad depicts the playing out of Willems's stream of consciousness:

He made a long stride, and saw her raise the revolver. . . .He saw a burst of red flame before his eyes, and was deafened by a report that seemed to him louder than a clap of thunder. Something stopped him short, and he stood aspiring in his nostrils the acrid smell of the blue smoke that drifted from before his eyes like an immense cloud. . . . Missed, by Heaven! . . . Thought so! . . . And he saw her very far off, throwing her arms up, while the revolver, very small, lay on the ground between them. . . . Missed! . . . He would go and pick it up now. Never before did he understand, as in that second, the joy, the triumphant delight of sunshine and of life. His mouth was full of something salt and warm. He tried to cough; spat out. . . .Who shrieks: In the name of God, he dies!— he dies!—Who dies?—Must pick up—Night!—What? . . . Night already.

Writing late in 1894 to Marguerite Poradowska, Conrad stated that the theme of *An Outcast of the Islands* was "the unrestrained, fierce vanity of an ignorant man who has had some success but neither principles nor any other line of conduct than the satisfaction of his vanity. In addition, he is not even faithful to himself."[5]

The novel winds down in a parodic theodicy in which Almayer asks a drinking companion why "such damned things" as stinging insects are made and scoundrels like Willems exist: "Where's your Providence? . . . The world's a swindle. . . . Why should I suffer? What have I done to be treated so?" A few lines of comedy follow and the book comes to an awkward close.

4

Ethical Agents Who Are Unaware: *The Nigger of the "Narcissus"* and *Typhoon*

In his first two novels, Joseph Conrad gave his chief attention to individuals who were victims of self-delusion and self-betrayal, whose consciousness was vitiated by an intense but false awareness of themselves as moral beings. Conrad's fictional world would continue to be heavily populated with such people, and his ironic vision never strayed away from them for long. In his third novel, however, Conrad's interest was drawn to another kind of individual, the ethical agent who is able without being particularly self-conscious of his powers. For such people the world is ordered so that their resources prove adequate for whatever they are required to do. Life never presents these lucky ones with a challenge beyond their moral and physical strength. They never become aware of moral incapacity. In Conrad's own term, they remain "unconscious."

Although his long career as a mariner apparently gave Conrad little satisfaction and a great deal of frustration, he did bring away experiences that would enrich his novels of the sea—especially *The Nigger of the "Narcissus"* (1897) and *Typhoon* (1902). And it seems no accident that Conrad found his prize specimens of the fortunate and able—and unconscious—among those he called "children of the sea."[1] From these two works, two examples will be considered: Old Singleton, able seaman of the sailing ship *Narcissus,* and Captain MacWhirr, who took the steamer *Nan-Shan* safely through the fury of a typhoon. Conrad's treatment of these uncon-

scious actors makes it clear that he looked upon them with
affection if not with total admiration.

Singleton

The Nigger of the "Narcissus" has been called a novel without
a hero. Conrad himself, in his note "To My Readers in America" (1914), stated that the title character, James Wait, "is
nothing; he is merely the centre of the ship's collective psychology and the pivot of the action." Curiously the author
did not there mention old Singleton, who I believe is the
novel's authentic hero. Throughout the double ordeal of
the *Narcissus* and her crew in facing the storm at sea and the
death of James Wait, old Singleton stands and endures. The
large space granted him and the extended word pictures of
the old seaman indicate that he was intended by his creator
to perform some unusual thematic duties.

When the new sailor Wait asks Singleton, "What kind of
ship is this?" Conrad pointedly editorializes that the wisdom
of half a century speaks "unconsciously" in Singleton's an-
swer: "Ship! . . . Ships are all right. It is the men in them!"

Here Conrad indulges in a rhetoric-laden digression cele-
brating "the everlasting children of the mysterious sea," a
passage that because of its unwonted nostalgia and flimsy
logic seems strangely out of keeping with the general tone of
this brief novel. He frees himself, and his readers, from this
peril of retrospective sentimentality by a piece of action involving Singleton. They are told that this "sixty-year-old
child" of the sea had been standing "meditative and unthinking"; but with a sailor's alert understanding of the emergency
he seizes the handle of the screw-brake and forces another
half-turn from the brake.

Conrad's viewpoint, at first that of an omniscient author,
suddenly shifts in the second chapter to that of crewman/
narrator.[2] In his note to American readers, Conrad said of
the novel: "Its pages are the tribute of my unalterable and
profound affection for the ships, the seamen, the winds and
the great sea—the moulders of my youth, the companions of
the best years of my life." Indeed, on the final page of the

novel, the identities of omniscient author and fellow crewman merge in a valedictory to the men of the *Narcissus:* "You were a good crowd. As good a crowd as ever fisted with wild cries the beating canvas of a heavy foresail; or tossing aloft, invisible in the night, gave back yell for yell to a westerly gale."

This sentiment, which might be acceptable ordinarily, led Conrad into an inconsistency that I think is far more serious than the matter of viewpoint. The logic of these nostalgic passages is shaky precisely because Conrad allowed his feeling to blur—at least momentarily—his vision of what actually went on aboard the *Narcissus.* The crewmen are characterized as "healthy and contented—as most seamen are, when once well out to sea." Then follows immediately the celebrated pronouncement:

The true peace of God begins at any spot a thousand miles from the nearest land; and when He sends there the messengers of His might it is not in terrible wrath against crime, presumption, and folly, but paternally, to chasten simple hearts—ignorant hearts that know nothing of life, and beat undisturbed by envy or greed.

It may be that the peace of God begins at any spot a thousand miles from the nearest land, but not if the *Narcissus* at that moment happens to be there! In view of Conrad's own testimony it becomes a choice between a serious lapse into sentimentality and, at the best, a clumsy handling of irony. Either way, once the spell of his hypnotic language is broken, it appears that Conrad was not completely successful in this portion of a work by which he wrote, in the 1914 note to American readers, that he was willing to stand or fall "as an artist striving for the utmost sincerity of expression."

For on the very next page of the novel, readers are told that the seamen "disputed endlessly, obstinate and childish," that the fanatical cook is "like a conceited saint," and that the mutinous Donkin sits on the forecastlehead "solitary and brooding over his wrongs." In chapter 2 where the book buckles with the sudden shift of viewpoint, the black seaman soon becomes the occasion of fighting and thievery. By the end of the chapter, James Wait, "worse than a nightmare," overshadows the ship: "Invulnerable in his promise of speedy corruption he trampled on our self-respect, he demonstrated to us daily our want of moral courage; he tainted our lives."

The peace of God?!

Chapter 3, containing Conrad's famous account of the storm, is a model of existential analysis, presenting the men's struggle with the sea as intensified by their ordeal in the rescue of James Wait, which the narrator says "had become a personal matter between us and the sea." Suspecting that Wait is malingering, the crewmen are torn between indignation and doubt:

We could not scorn him safely—neither could we pity him without risk to our dignity. . . . The secret and ardent desire of our hearts was the desire to beat him viciously with our fists about the head; and we handled him as tenderly as though he had been made of glass.

The psychological analysis continues. Although the storm begins to subside, the men cannot "spare a moment or a thought from the great mental occupation of wishing to live." They bear "the pain of existence" until dawn comes, while Singleton hangs on at the wheel "with open and lifeless eyes."

Conrad's artful focus on Singleton at the chapter's conclusion reminds us how remarkably the old seaman has dominated the book so far. Chapter 1 ended with a symbolic and masterful act, and the words "You . . . hold!" A dominant note of chapter 2 was sounded in Singleton's advice to Wait to get on with his dying; and, although the crew refused to believe in Wait's death, Singleton assured them, "Why, of course he will die." Now chapter 3 ends with the famous words—"He steered with care."

Conrad prefaces chapter 4 with a paragraph heavily charged with rhetoric and irony stating a point that writers of recent fashion have been iterating in various ways: the melancholy fact that the life of all human beings is "redeemed" at last by death. After more than thirty hours at the wheel, old Singleton steps through the door into the forecastle, and to the consternation of his mates, falls forward, "crashing down, stiff and headlong like an uprooted tree." Although he later returns to duty, the effect of Singeton's encounter with mortal fatigue is suggested as he broods: "Like a man bound treacherously while he sleeps, he woke up fettered by the long chain of disregarded years," and he knows the "pitiless vastness" of the sea will claim his own worn-out body.

Earlier in the novel Conrad described the *Narcissus* as like "a small planet," surrounded by "the abysses of sky and sea," bearing "an intolerable load of regrets and hopes . . . timid truth and audacious lies." Now, as she sails homeward, he supplies a new inventory of the ship's cargo: She carries the crewmen's "conceited folly" and Singleton's "completed wisdom": the sinister truth that he too is mortal.

Nevertheless, in the affirmative routine of activity that follows the failure of Donkin's mutiny, old Singleton remains the symbol of tireless and faithful service. The final apotheosis of Singleton comes when he announces that Wait will die in sight of land. So far as the crewmen are concerned, Singleton "radiated unspeakable wisdom. . . . Round him all the listeners felt themselves somehow completely enlightened." Conrad pronounces him to be "profound and unconscious."

Finally, the first land in four months is sighted, and Jim Wait, stolen for by Belfast, lied to by all the crew except Singleton, stolen from at the last by Donkin, dies. After the lugubrious ritual of committing Wait's shrouded corpse to the sea, a fair wind arises; and " 'What did I tell you?' mumbled old Singleton; . . . 'I knowed it—he's gone, and here it comes.' "

The ship sails home to England, and Conrad, taking leave of the crew of the *Narcissus,* asks, "Haven't we, together and upon the immortal sea, wrung out a meaning from our sinful lives?" Perhaps "we" have wrung out a meaning from our sinful lives. It is less certain that Singleton derived much "meaning" from his life. Along with the other crewmen of the *Narcissus* he shared the "pain of existence," and he "knew how to exist," which meant without doubts or hopes. To his fellow seamen he seemed, on occasion, to possess "a sharper

vision, a clearer knowledge." But Conrad drastically circum-
scribes the limits of his vision and knowledge. Singleton suffers from prickly heat, he understands physical hardships, he
is acquainted with his captain's temper, he knows that ships
are all right—"It is the men in them!"—he acknowledges the
invincibility of wind and sea, he surrenders to fatigue, and
he realizes that he will die. In Conrad's view, that is all he
knows or needs to know on land or sea.

In a letter to R. B. Cunninghame Graham (Dec. 14, 1897),
Conrad wrote on this point:

If it is the knowledge of how to live, my man [Singleton] essentially possessed it. He was in perfect accord with his life. . . . Would
you seriously, of malice prepense cultivate in that unconscious man
the power to think? Then he would become conscious—and much
smaller—and very unhappy. Now he is simple and great like an
elemental force. Nothing can touch him but the curse of decay—
the eternal decree that will extinguish the sun, the stars one by one,
and in another instant shall spread a frozen darkness over the whole
universe. Nothing else can touch him—he does not think.
Would you seriously wish to tell such a man: "Know thyself".
Understand that thou art nothing, less than a shadow, more insignificant than a drop of water in the ocean, more fleeting than the
illusion of a dream. Would you?[3]

Some critics of Conrad have denied that his art is touched
by nihilism.[4] Granting that one might overlook the grim implications buried in the rhetoric of the novel itself, it is hard
to ignore the meaning of this private comment written within
weeks of the book's publication. At any rate, the letter gives
an indication why, throughout the novel, Conrad arranged
for Singleton to remain "unheeding," "ever unthinking,"
"untouched by human emotions," "profound and unconscious."

MacWhirr of *Typhoon*

The second unconscious actor to be considered in this chapter
is Captain Thomas MacWhirr, who appeared in *Typhoon*, a
short novel Conrad completed soon after he finished "Heart

of Darkness" and *Lord Jim*. Nearly twenty years later, in an author's note, he summarized this "bit of sea yarn" as an affair of bad weather assailing a steamship full of Chinese passengers, with the ship's life complicated "at a moment of exceptional stress by the human element below her deck." What had been needed, wrote Conrad, was "a leading motive that would harmonize all these violent noises, and a point of view that would put all that elemental fury into its proper place." He added: "What was needed of course was Captain MacWhirr."

In the story itself, the omniscient narrator proceeds with a comically ironic portrayal of MacWhirr: "Having just enough imagination to carry him through each successive day, and no more, he was tranquilly sure of himself; and from the very same cause he was not in the least conceited." Now in the prime of his career, Captain MacWhirr has an eye for duty, of course, and also for "facts."

He notes, for example, the fact that a brand-new lock on the *Nan-Shan* is defective, and he makes a simple inference leading to another fact: "You can't trust the workmen nowadays." It is MacWhirr's faith, based on years of meditating facts, that "there's just so much dirty weather knocking about the world." "Faithful to facts," he writes home twelve times a year, letters that relate "in minute detail each successive trip of the *Nan-Shan*" to a wife whose only secret is "her abject terror of the time when her husband would come home to stay for good."

The literal-minded MacWhirr amuses his first mate, who believes that it is "not worth while trying to impress a man of that sort." And, Conrad adds, "The sea itself, as if sharing Mr. Jukes' good-natured forbearance, had never put itself out to startle the silent man, who . . . wandered innocently over the waters."

Conrad's first chapter, which began in comic irony, now ends by modulating to symbolic statement embracing man-made as well as natural evil:

Captain MacWhirr had sailed over the surface of the oceans as some men go skimming over the years of existence to sink gently into a placid grave, ignorant of life to the last, without ever having been made to see all it may contain of perfidy, of violence, and of terror. There are on sea and land such men thus fortunate—or thus disdained by destiny or by the sea.

What must be understood here is that Conrad's conception of MacWhirr embraces a dual deficiency in the man. He is limited in his comprehension of the variety and complexity of evils outside his own experience. And this moral isolation has preserved his innocence that, reinforced by his defective imagination, has kept him *unaware* of his own potential connection with evil. Paradoxically, MacWhirr will be made to triumph by virtue of this deficiency, linked to his great good luck and steadfastness. Evil will assert itself in the murderous fury of the typhoon, in the normal fears of Jukes, in the crazy cowardice of the second mate, in the paralysis of the crew, in the panic of the passengers. "Never heard a lot of coolies spoken of as passengers before," says MacWhirr. But he will harmonize "all these violent noises" and put "all that elemental fury in its proper place" without ever really relating himself to evil in a significant way.[5]

When the storm comes on, Jukes is "uncritically glad" to have his captain in charge. MacWhirr, certainly not intended as a ludicrous distortion in these pages, is represented as bearing the very human burden and "the loneliness of command." At the height of the storm the boatswain reports disaster in the hold where two hundred Chinese passengers, with their possessions scattered by the violent tossing, are trapped in a mortal frenzy. After a scene subtly grotesque in its comedy,[6] the mate is sent down to investigate. MacWhirr remains on the bridge and nerves the terrified helmsman and, when the crazed second mate rushes him, he neatly knocks him unconscious. Jukes, exceedingly reluctant to do his duty by the coolies, nevertheless reports through the speakingtube to his captain, who seems like "an enlightened comprehension dwelling alone up there with a storm." The "voice that kept the hurricane out of Jukes's ear" orders him to take the crewmen and pick up the silver dollars spilled from the coolies' smashed boxes. This they manage to do by the time the ship enters the eye of the storm, and to the satisfaction of MacWhirr, who is determined to "do what's fair by them."

The captain enters the wrecked chartroom, gropes for a box of matches. His reading of the instruments tells him that the worst is yet to come. The scrupulous captain returns the matches to their accustomed place, "but before he removed his hand it occurred to him that perhaps he would never have occasion to use that box any more. The vividness of the thought checked him and for an infinitesimal fraction of a second his fingers closed again on the small object as though it had been the symbol of all these little habits that chain us to the weary round of life." So far from caricature is this man of "unseeing, unimaginative" ways. Like the "unconscious" Singleton, he acknowledges the idea of death.

The end of the chapter, wherein Conrad adroitly avoids an artist's impossible task of describing the second half of the storm, is masterfully understated. The hurricane

had found this taciturn man in its path, and, doing its utmost, had managed to wring out a few words. Before the renewed wrath of the winds swooped on his ship, Captain MacWhirr was moved to declare, in a tone of vexation, as it were: "I wouldn't like to lose her."

He was spared that annoyance.

Typhoon ends as it began, in a mood of comic irony. Conrad views MacWhirr indulgently, sympathetically: but his judgment seems to tally with that of Jukes, who held that the old man "got out of it very well for such a stupid man." Under the irony, behind the grotesquerie, is Conrad's serious judgment against a man who may know that defective locks are made by defective men, that a typhoon and death itself can overwhelm puny human beings, that these human beings can endanger the safety of one another, yet in a sublimity of innocence can remain unaware of the true nature of evil. Such a man, Conrad seems to be saying, is disdained by destiny if not by the sea.

5

Tragic Awareness—Marlow

Conrad's fiction thus far has been peopled with characters who are falsely aware, or with those who are essentially unaware of a tragic dimension in their own lives. In his two earliest novels, Almayer and Willems maintained an illusory view of reality that rendered them incapable of tragic awareness. Such characters continued to call forth Conrad's scorn in other works throughout his writing life.

In Conrad's third novel, "unconscious" Singleton, the old seaman of the *Narcissus,* and, later in *Typhoon,* Captain MacWhirr, responded to challenge with straightforward and unselfconscious actions. In both cases, personal ability and good fortune conspired to defend them from full and tragic awareness.[1]

This chapter and the succeeding chapter will consider some works of Conrad's great middle period, works that have earned critical esteem largely by virtue of his success in sounding the psychological depths of characters who are endowed with the intelligence to understand their responsible involvement in a moral universe. In characters like Marlow of *Lord Jim* and "Heart of Darkness," and Mrs. Gould, of *Nostromo,* resides a conviction of personal freedom chastened by tragic knowledge that this freedom can be thwarted by deficiencies within as well as without. These characters are tragic because they are fully and truly conscious. Tragic awareness comes to them when they realize their moral inadequacy, their inability even in the face of great obligation to control their intentions or the consequence of their actions.

Marlow

Lord Jim (1900) is generally regarded as Joseph Conrad's most complex book. Its structure depends more than that of any other Conrad work upon the multiple viewpoints of its characters, and the result is what Albert Guerard called "the first novel in a new form: a form bent on involving and implicating the reader in a psycho-moral drama which has no easy solution."[2]

Marlow is the chief narrator, set in a frame of limited knowledge introduced by an unnamed "I," and other narrators are routed through Marlow's consciousness.

This Marlow has probably been the subject of more critical comment than any other creation of Conrad, and this is so because he stands simultaneously as the Conrad character par excellence and as the epitome of the Conrad novelistic technique. Marlow is at once a creation and a device. What has sometimes clouded some of the critical comment has been the failure to demonstrate clearly that while Marlow becomes the hallmark of an evolving technique (which by the way is not confined to the stories in which he appears by name), even when he appears under the name, he is not one and the same character.[3] To put it another way, Marlow begins and ends as a device, in "Youth" and in a later novel, *Chance*. Only in *Lord Jim* and in "Heart of Darkness" is he the remarkable character who possesses a complex and tentative view of a complex and ambiguous world. But before examining Conrad's achievement in *Lord Jim* and "Heart of Darkness," I propose to trace Marlow's provisional beginning in "Youth" and his commonplace end in *Chance*.

"Youth"

Jocelyn Baines linked the origin of Marlow to Conrad's frustration at being unable to complete his third book dealing with Lingard, previously noted in chapter 1 as "The Rescuer"; and he further hypothesizes that Conrad's friend Cunninghame Graham at this time suggested a try at writing something closer to his own experience.[4] Someone or something

seems also to have encouraged Conrad to try a more colloquial style. At any rate, in the fall of 1898, *Blackwood's
Magazine* published a narrative called "Youth" and Marlow
was introduced to the world.

The fact is that two Marlows are presented in this brief
piece, which is so obviously rooted in the experience of Conrad's own youth. The mature seaman Marlow recounts to
his listeners an event of twenty-two years earlier when he was
an untested second officer of twenty on the ill-fated *Judea*.
The explicit theme of the story, presented with indulgent irony
by the older man, is the vast gulf in time and experience
between the callow young shipman he was—romantically
avid for adventure, exhilarated at finding he could endure
danger and disaster—and the Marlow who has been matured
by life's disenchantments. Marlow is introduced in "Youth,"
as he will be in "Heart of Darkness," with his audience of
four, including an unnamed narrator. He is a vivid raconteur,
colloquial, meditative, at times ironic, at other times sentimental. But in "Youth" there is no moral or psychological
struggle for Marlow and, consequently, there is no struggle
for the reader.

Chance

Nor does the Marlow of *Chance* (1914) struggle in self-con-
flict, though present-day readers of Conrad's first "popular"
novel may have a struggle with their patience as they pick
their way through needlessly intricate Marlovian machinery.[5]

In the Marlow (and the Conrad) of *Chance,* I find a new
and disappointing tone that hesitates between coyness and
ponderous self-certainty. For this new Marlow, little is tentative or ambiguous in the world of truth and reality. Even
when speaking of the unforeseen results of human conduct,
he does so with a pedantic, almost lip-smacking assurance:
"It's certainly unwise to admit any sort of responsibility for
our actions. . . . And perhaps it's just as well, since, for the
most part, we cannot be certain of the effect of our actions."
"Certainly . . . we cannot be certain." This is not purposeful
paradox but, I think, debilitated, self-parodying rhetoric. In

an effort to lighten the effect of such platitudinizing, Conrad manages it so that the unnamed narrator who finds Marlow at times "vehement," "pessimistic," "earnestly cynical," is made to ask Marlow: "Do you really believe what you have said?" And Marlow answers with a malicious smile: "Only on certain days of the year."

Actually, there is about the whole novel a strain of levity that causes the character to become another personality than the Marlow of *Lord Jim* and "Heart of Darkness," for the persistently comic tone, which Conrad here appears to have sought, is that which accompanies settled convictions. Comedy may serviceably attack poses of righteousness and truth. But, in spite of recent achievements in forms of black farce, comedy does not seem to be the best mode in which to explore the tragic ambivalences of righteousness and truth.

In the author's note written almost a decade after the novel, Conrad, after denying a "didactic" intent in his fiction, concluded with an exculpatory air exactly recalling the pompous dictum of the new Marlow: "It is only for their intentions that men can be held responsible. The ultimate effects of whatever they do are far beyond their control." This statement is doubly disappointing. From it, in the first place, proceeds Conrad's astonishing avowal concerning his own "blameless" intentions in writing *Chance*. What is sadder, perhaps, is that by this lapse Conrad implicitly betrayed his brilliant achievement with Marlow in "Heart of Darkness" and in *Lord Jim*.

It is now time to explore the nature of that achievement.

Lord Jim

Thomas Moser a good while ago perceived the special force of Marlow as a character and as a literary device. Particularly he saw Marlow as identifying with Jim's dilemma and also, as interviewer, bringing together and evaluating the testimony of secondary observers of Jim. Conrad's art, he declared, "lies in the way he carefully qualifies each narrator's analysis of Jim and shows clearly that the truth about Jim must be the sum of many perceptions."[6]

Albert Guerard, as indicated earlier in this chapter, found in *Lord Jim* a new fictional form—evolving midway between Melville's "Benito Cereno" and Faulkner's *Absalom, Absalom!* This new form, which Guerard denominated the psychomoral novel, while seeking to engage the reader's sensibilities "more strenuously and even more uncomfortably than ever before," forces upon the reader "an active exploratory, organizing role," with the consequence that the reader finds himself to be a collaborator in the writing of the novel.[7]

Conrad, Marlow, and the reader then must be seen as participants in a total drama of moral and psychological ambiguity. What will be examined here will be the scope of Marlow's knowledge and the depth of his tragic awareness. Marlow, I believe, can be trusted as Conrad's spokesman when it is a matter of reporting event or stating fact, but readers should be alert to subjective judgments on Marlow's part, especially, as I will show later, regarding his view of Stein. Marlow's appeal is in the marvelous way his intelligence presents the "facts" as colored by his subtly shifting feelings, as well as by the multiple attitudes of other witnesses that filter through his consciousness. Marlow's ways of presenting evidence and testimony in Jim's case, his own involvement in judgment upon and sympathy with Jim, all combine to indicate the extent of Marlow's insight into the tragic nature of awareness beyond one's ability to escape responsibility or complicity.

The unnamed narrator, in chapter 4, before turning the story over to Marlow, remarks that "later on, many times, in distant parts of the world, Marlow showed himself willing to remember Jim, to remember him at length, in detail and audibly." The problem is to notice how, in his remembering of Jim, the details shape themselves into meaning for Marlow. A clue to Marlow's meaning comes early in his narrative to his unprotesting listeners: he has a familiar devil, he tells them, which "causes me to run up against men with soft spots, with hard spots, with hidden plague spots, by Jove! and loosens their tongues at the sight of me for their infernal confidences; . . . as though—God help me!—I didn't have

enough confidential information about myself to harrow my
own soul till the end of my appointed time."

Marlow's first view of Jim comes on the day when Jim and
the other officers of the *Patna* were brought safely to port,
unaware that the abandoned vessel has been miraculously
saved with all its eight hundred passengers. Marlow feels that
the young deserter "had no business to look so sound"; yet
he concedes that "not one of us is safe" from "weakness
unknown, . . . repressed or maybe ignored more than half a
lifetime." Jim, he says, was "one of us," standing for men
and women with instinctive courage—

I mean just that inborn ability to look temptations straight in the
face—a readiness unintellectual enough, . . . an unthinking and
blessed stiffness before the outward and inward terrors, before the
might of nature, and the seductive corruption of men—backed by
a faith invulnerable to the strength of facts, to the contagion of
example, to the solicitation of ideas.

Two things Marlow cannot know—one, that he is solemnly
echoing Conrad's knowledgeable narrator, who earlier had
ironically introduced a leitmotif of the novel with the comment that Jim, early in his apprenticeship, "felt angry with
the brutal tumult of earth and sky for taking him unawares
and checking unfairly a generous readiness for narrow es-
capes"; and, two, that he, Marlow, is expressing admiration
for precisely the type of unconscious personality for whom
Singleton and MacWhirr were Conrad's early and esteemed
models. Marlow now desires to learn the truth behind the
facts in Jim's case, perhaps to find "some profound and re-
deeming cause, some merciful explanation, some convincing
shadow of an excuse."

The time arrives for the official inquiry, and Marlow introduces the first of his subordinate witnesses, Captain
Brierly, a member of the court of inquiry. Here the reader
must be alerted to the limits of Marlow's knowledge of fact,
and at the same time sense the incipient sarcasm in his tone.
So far as Marlow knows, Brierly "had never in his life made

a mistake, never had an accident, never a mishap, never a check in his steady rise, and he seemed to be one of those lucky fellows who know nothing of indecision, much less of self-mistrust."

But, very soon after the inquiry, Brierly commits suicide, and Marlow is obliged to revise his opinion. He concludes that Brierly, who had been severely judgmental of Jim, "was probably holding silent inquiry into his own case," and that he took a guilty secret of disgrace with him "in that leap into the sea."[8] Marlow wonders "what flattering view he had induced himself to take of his own suicide."[9]

As the novel progresses, each new witness similarly will provide Marlow with means to achieve new insights into Jim and into himself. The next witness, however, is Jim who gives his own version of the *Patna* affair. Marlow's account of the interview begins with one of the book's many variations on the theme: "He was one of us."

For Jim presses Marlow with an urgent question: "Do you know what *you* would have done? Do you?" Marlow says Jim was "too much like one of us not to be dangerous." He realizes that what Jim is asking for is not a listener to judge him—"He wanted an ally, a helper, an accomplice."[10] Jim insists that he did not think of saving himself. His only thought had been "eight hundred people and seven boats—and not time!" Marlow accepts this, but Jim's imagination, this "faculty of swift and forestalling vision" that unmanned him, is pointedly contrasted with the faithful stolidity of the two lascars who remained at their posts.

Conrad's magnificent chapter 9 begins with Jim's account of his experience on the *Patna*—isolated from the passengers and the other crew members, repeating to himself, "Sink—curse you! Sink!" Marlow says that at the same time Jim "enjoyed the privilege of witnessing scenes . . . of low comedy."

Jim recalls the ludicrous sight of the four officers struggling to release a stubborn lifeboat: "I ought to have a merry life of it, by God! for I shall see that funny sight a good many times yet before I die." Then the donkey-man, acting third engineer, had slid to a sitting posture, dead of excitement and overexertion—"Droll, isn't it . . . fooled into killing himself!" The engineer's death Jim pronounces "a joke hatched in hell."

Marlow believes that throughout the tumult of events and sensations Jim had preserved "a strange illusion of passiveness, as though he had not acted but had suffered himself to be handled by the infernal powers who had selected him for the victim of their practical joke." But was Jim's decision totally unfree? Marlow is skeptical: "The infernal joke was being crammed devilishly down his throat, but—look you— he was not going to admit of any sort of swallowing motion in his gullet."

The three officers in the lifeboat had called to the lifeless engineer on deck, and only Jim had heard the shout—

"Eight hundred living people, and they were yelling after the one dead man to come down and be saved. . . . 'Jump, George! We'll catch you!' . . . The ship began a slow plunge; . . . 'Geo-o-o-orge! Oh, jump!' She was going down, down, head first under me. . . ." He raised his hand deliberately to his face, and made picking motions with his fingers as though he had been bothered with cobwebs, and afterwards he looked into the open palm for quite half a second before he blurted out— "I had jumped . . ." He checked himself, averted his gaze. . . . "It seems," he added.

Marlow's next interview is with an elderly French naval lieutenant he met in Sidney "a long time after," who turned out to be one of the boarding officers who had taken the abandoned *Patna* in tow. Marlow judges him to be "one of those steady, reliable men who are the raw material of great reputations." Significantly, Marlow says he *looked* like "a reliable officer."

The lieutenant expounds "with stolid glibness" how they had taken the derelict in tow, stern foremost to ease the strain of the imperiled bulkhead— "*éxigeait les plus grands ménagements.*" Then, "priest-like," he listens to Marlow's story of Jim. In response, he expatiates on the topic of fear: "One is always afraid. . . . One puts up with it." He concludes: "But the honour . . . that is real—that is! And what life may be worth when . . . when the honour is gone—*ah ça! par ex-*

emple—I can offer no opinion. I can offer no opinion—because—monsieur—I know nothing of it."

With this speech the French lieutenant rests his case, and
Marlow admits defeat. But, just possibly, more was intended
by Conrad, more than Marlow seems to realize, more than
critics generally have recognized in Conrad's subtle treatment.[11] This lieutenant who to Marlow "looked a reliable
officer"—could it be that even while he discoursed on honor,
a guilty memory threatened to assert itself? The lieutenant
had said that for all fear is sure to come—"the fear of themselves." And he had added, "Absolutely so. Trust me." Should
not a close reader of Conrad be alerted by this positive as-
sertion of human certitude? The lieutenant had continued:

> "Yes. Yes. . . . At my age one knows what one is talking about—
> *que diable!*" . . . He had delivered himself of all this as immovably
> as though he had been the mouthpiece of abstract wisdom, but at
> this point he heightened the effect of detachment by beginning to
> twirl his thumbs slowly. "It's evident— *parbleu!*" he continued;
> "for, make up your mind as much as you like, even a simple head-
> ache or a fit of indigestion *(un dérangement d'estomac)* is enough
> to . . . Take me, for instance—I have made my proofs. *Eh bien!* I,
> who am speaking to you, once . . ."

Marlow reports that "he drained his glass and returned to
his twirling. 'No, no; one does not die of it,' he pronounced,
finally, and when I found he did not mean to proceed with
the personal anecdote, I was extremely disappointed."

Marlow, disconcerted by the lieutenant's stern pronouncement on honor, asks, of the matter of honor, "Couldn't it
reduce itself to not being found out?" Conrad lets the un-
suspecting Marlow report: "He made as if to retort readily,
but when he spoke he had changed his mind. 'This, monsieur,
is too fine for me—much above me—I don't think about it.'"
After an almost comic ceremony of bowing and scraping, the
lieutenant walks out of Marlow's life forever.

Marlow, "alone and discouraged" after the lieutenant's
departure, sits thinking now of "little Bob Stanton," whose
heroism was certified by his death trying to save a passenger
in a shipwreck. Then, following the court's adjournment,

Marlow is confronted by the incarnation of another way of looking at Jim. Chester, who had been "everything a man may be at sea, but a pirate," offers to take Jim on for a job on a remote guano island. Marlow angrily refuses to help persuade Jim to go. Chester is disappointed: "He is no earthly good for anything. . . . He would just have done for me. . . . Anyhow, I could guarantee the island wouldn't sink under him—and I believe he is a bit particular on that point."

Following the inquiry Jim makes a progressive retreat Eastward as the scandal pursues him from job to job. Eventually, Marlow—made handy by Conrad—takes Jim away, and on his behalf goes to Stein for help.

In considering the implications of Marlow's interview with Stein, readers should proceed carefully. In view of Conrad's penchant for doubling characters and incidents, it is worth recalling Marlow's earlier coments when Jim looked to *him* for help. Marlow remarked then: "I don't know how old I appeared to him—and how much wise." And he had concluded ironically that Jim "was there before me, believing that age and wisdom can find a remedy against the pain of truth."

Now Marlow confides his difficulty (and Jim's) to the old and wise Stein—"one of the most trustworthy men I had ever known." And many readers and some critics have been taken in by Marlow's judgment of Stein, feeling that Marlow tells him Jim's story because he is so wise. In view of the oracular obscurity of the old man's counsel and the ultimately disastrous results of his practical remedy for Jim's "romantic" malady, it seems safer to say that Marlow tells Stein Jim's story because he *thinks* Stein is so wise.

In Marlow's judgment, "this Stein"—a wealthy and respectable merchant—"possessed an intrepidity of spirit and a physical courage that could have been called reckless had it not been like a natural function of the body—say good digestion, for instance—completely unconscious of itself." Marlow is thus made to bring Stein's psychology close to that of Singleton and MacWhirr. In other words, Stein was able and fortunate without being unduly self-conscious. So far, Marlow's view might be considered to parallel Conrad's view of Stein. There seems to be no reason to question Marlow's judgment here any more than there is to doubt his factual account of the career of "this merchant, adventurer, sometime adviser of a Malay sultan" who had achieved an international distinction for his collection of beetles and butterflies. But in chapter 20 Stein begins to speak for himself and the reader must now be alert to Stein's self-revelatory clues.

His first words to Marlow—"So you see me—so"—betoken a harmless vanity in the old man. Hovering among his butterfly cases, he comments on his specimens with engaging directness. He tells Marlow how he caught a rare specimen and "had a very big emotion." He was, he says, riding alone when a volley of shots came at him from ambush. Significantly, his words echo an idiom of the French lieutenant: "I see it all in a minute and I think———This wants a little management." Stein outwits his enemies, kills three of them, and the others flee. Then, as he tells Marlow, he spies a shadow passing over one of the corpses. He recognizes a rare species of butterfly as it flutters away, but it stops on a small heap of dirt and he captures it. As he recounts his triumph, the old man is possessed by emotion again. Recovering, he invites Marlow to speak his business.

Although he had considered Stein to be "an eminently suitable person" to hear his story, Marlow now hesitates "on the brink of confidence," filled with "all sorts of doubts." Is this a hint from Conrad that Stein's advice may be inadequate?

Marlow reports that following Stein's diagnosis of Jim's "case," he asked, "What's good for it?" and Stein "lifted up a long forefinger. 'There is only one remedy! One thing alone can us from being ourselves cure!' The finger came down on the desk with a smart rap." This eloquent sign of death, Marlow reports, made Jim's case "still simpler—and altogether hopeless." After a pause Marlow says, "Yes, . . . strictly speaking, the question is not how to get cured, but how to live." And Stein agrees: "That is the question. . . . How to be! *Ach!* How to be."

Now the old German, who had been a lucky and able adventurer, whose youth (if one can trust Marlow and Conrad) was filled with unreflecting activity, tries his hand at philosophizing. His allusion to Shakespeare is obvious. He has already quoted from Goethe. It appears from what follows that he (as well as his creator Conrad) was familiar with Calderón de la Barca's *La Vida es Sueño*. But Stein is not the key to Conrad's own mind, as some have thought.[12] Nor is he Conrad's unique "god" figure who can "order human destinies through his superior wisdom and infinite capabilities."[13] Instead, he will prove to be another of Conrad's failed agents of Providence.

Nor, indeed, does Conrad's presentation of Stein point to "a major and sentimental uncertainty in the author," as Guerard suspected.[14] On the contrary, I believe that Conrad the artist works carefully here to present an aged man's persistence in a worldview that, while romantic, is scarcely deeper in its psycho-moral dimension than was the vision of Singleton or MacWhirr. Recall that the unconscious Singleton at times seemed, in the eyes of his fellow seamen, "as wise as he looked," and to possess "a sharper vision, a clearer knowledge." To the imaginative Jukes, Captain MacWhirr was like "an enlightened comprehension dwelling alone up there with a storm." Both Singleton and MacWhirr fell short of tragic knowledge. Does Stein, despite Marlow's opinion (and that of many critics), prove to be any more truly aware?

Stein does at one moment appear to stand on the threshold of tragic knowledge. He goes so far as to verbalize the formula: awareness beyond ability. To Marlow he discourses: "We want in so many different ways to be. . . . This magnificent butterfly finds a little heap of dirt and sits still on it; but man he will never on his heap of mud keep still."

This analogy marks a sentimental lapse on Stein's part, for no butterfly remains on its heap of dirt; in fact, this butterfly was captured precisely because it *did* sit still on its dirt heap. Stein continues: "He wants to be a saint, and he wants to be a devil—and every time he shuts his eyes he sees himself as a very fine fellow—so fine as he can never be. . . . In a dream."

Marlow is made to picture Stein, priestlike and mysterious, as he closes the butterfly case: "And taking up the case in both hands he bore it religiously away to its place, passing out of the bright circle of the lamp into the ring of fainter light—into shapeless dusk at last." Recalling that the French lieutenant, a less than trustworthy witness,[15] conjured up in Marlow's mind the image of a priest, one might guess that Conrad is here hinting that Stein is a fallible agent of Providence. At any rate, Stein proceeds to state the tragic formula, at first with confidence:

And because you not always can keep your eyes shut there comes the real trouble—the heart pain—the world pain. I tell you, my friend, it is not good for you to find you cannot make your dream come true, for the reason that you not strong enough are, or not clever enough.

The old man continues:

A man that is born falls into a dream like a man who falls into the sea. If he tries to climb out into the air as inexperienced people endeavor to do, he drowns— *nicht wahr?* No! I tell you. The way is to the destructive element submit yourself and with the exertions of your hands and feet in the water make the deep, deep sea keep you up. So if you ask me—how to be?

Marlow reports (and there is no reason to doubt his verbal accuracy) that Stein's voice "leaped up extraordinarily strong, as though away there in the dusk he had been inspired by some whisper of knowledge. 'I will tell you! For that, too, there is only one way.' "

Paradoxically, as the old man moves from the shadows he becomes less sure of himself. Stein

loomed up in the ring of faint light, and suddenly appeared in the bright circle of the lamp. His extended hand aimed at my breast like a pistol [portentous symbol!—C.D.B.]; his deep-set eyes seemed to pierce through me, but his twitching lips uttered no word, and the austere exaltation of a certitude seen in the dusk vanished from his face.

Stein's concluding speech, interestingly, contains the Latin motto that Conrad's Uncle Tadeusz Bobrowski once wrote in a letter to his "visionary" nephew. Just possibly, Joseph Conrad, although he loved and respected his mother's brother, here indulged himself in gentle satire of his uncle's viewpoint.

He spoke in a subdued tone, without looking at me, one hand on each side of his face. "That was the way. To follow the dream, and again to follow the dream—and so— *ewig—usque ad finem*. . . ." The whisper of his conviction seemed to open before me a vast and uncertain expanse, as of a crepuscular horizon on a plain at dawn—or was it, perchance, at the coming of the night? One had not the courage to decide.

Marlow's analysis of Stein continues: "His life had begun in sacrifice, in enthusiasm for generous ideas; he had travelled very far, on various ways, on strange paths, and whatever he followed it had been without faltering, and therefore without shame and without regret. In so far he was right." In other words, Stein's way is all right for the lucky and the able, those who though "romantic" like Stein are unselfconscious (as Jim was not), those whose tragic consciousness has never been awakened by the kind of failure (or knowledge of failure) that relates one, in tragic awareness, to evil.

Stein ends the interview by inviting Marlow to spend the night, and as host precedes guest, lighting the dark house, Marlow succumbs to the atmosphere, allows his mind to entertain romantic thoughts, and the talk verges on the sentimental:

"Yes," I said, as though carrying on a discussion, "and amongst other things you dreamed foolishly of a certain butterfly; but when one fine morning your dream came in your way you did not let the splendid opportunity escape. Did you? Whereas he . . ."

At Marlowe's reference to Jim, Stein lifts his hand—

"And do you know how many opportunities I let escape; how many dreams I had lost that had come in my way?" He shook his head regretfully. "It seems to me that some would have been very fine—

if I had made them come true. Do you know how many? Perhaps I myself don't know."

Later Marlow will express his dissatisfaction with Stein's inability to say more than that Jim was "romantic," but he does not now appear to notice Stein's vagueness and superficiality, because he is so intent on Jim's problem: " 'Whether his were fine or not,' I said, 'he knows of one which he certainly did not catch.' 'Everybody knows of one or two like that,' said Stein; 'and that is the trouble—the great trouble.' "

Now it is perfectly all right for an escaped butterfly to serve as a symbol (as here, indubitably, it does) for a lost opportunity. Stein admits to having let such opportunities escape. But what is the evidence that Stein's lost opportunities were any of them as fateful as Jim's lost chance on the *Patna?* Recalling Stein's ambush adventure, one may take a second look at his own testimony that his "big emotion" was occasioned not by his close escape from death but by his capture of the butterfly.

Assuming that he understood his own emotional responses, Stein's order of opportunities seized or lost might seem trivial compared with Jim's experience of lost honor on the *Patna* and his coming ordeal in Patusan. There is no hint anywhere that Stein's loss of friends or loved ones was regarded by him or anyone else as involving his responsibility. On the contrary, Marlow's account would indicate that Stein had always been able and self-sufficient, with no moral entanglements to betray weakness or produce guilt. The evidence is that Stein has been fortunate, unselfconscious if not unconscious, and that he remains tragically unaware.

Jim, falsely aware at the beginning of his career, encountered on the *Patna* a grim aspect of himself such as Stein presumably never knew about his own self; and in Patusan, by the help of Stein as it happens, Jim will recover his romantic image of himself. The sentimental talk ends with Stein bidding Marlow goodnight and going back to his butterflies after promising, "And tomorrow we must do something practical—practical."

It would seem that if the reader were not already alerted

to the psychodramatic implications of a novel that proceeds
on the basis of multiple viewpoints, the contemplation of
Stein's plan for Jim and its catastrophic results would raise
doubts concerning Stein's alleged godlike wisdom and ability.
Perhaps the only remedy for life *is* to submit oneself to the
destructive element. Jim's case proves, however, that such
immersion may lead to death. Or, to employ Stein's other
metaphor, to follow the dream may be to descend into a
nightmare.

It was Stein who provided Jim with his second chance by
making him his agent in Patusan. It is in Stein's house and
from the old man, together with Jewel and Tamb' Itam, that
Marlow hears of Jim's final disaster. It was Stein's ring that
carried Jim to Doramin, the Bugis chieftain. It was also Stein's
ring that became the symbol of Jim's unwitting betrayal of
Dain Waris, the old chief's son and Jim's closest friend. It
was the same silver ring that rolled from Doramin's lap when
he stood to confront Jim, and Jim watched the ring as it rolled
against his foot. Then, "while Jim stood stiffened and with
bared head in the light of torches, looking him straight in the
face, [Doramin] clung heavily with his left arm round the
neck of a bowed youth, and lifting deliberately his right, shot
his son's friend through the chest."

It may be useful to recall Stein's pointing his hand at Marlow's chest "like a pistol." The image occurred, two hundred
pages earlier, at the moment Stein came out of the shadows
to propose his "remedy" for Jim. It may be useful also to
note that Conrad plans it so that Stein has the last word on
the last page of the novel. Marlow reports to the "privileged
man" that "Stein has aged greatly of late. He feels it himself,
and says often that he is 'preparing to leave all this; preparing
to leave . . . while he waves his hands sadly at his butterflies."

There yet remain two witnesses to assist Marlow in his
appraisal of Jim's character: Jewel and Gentleman Brown.
The first of these, Jim's half-caste love, Marlow meets in
Patusan. She subjects Marlow to a painful catechism, and he
is obliged to equivocate in Jim's defense. Later, after the catastrophe has taken the lives of Dain Waris and Lord Jim,
the bitter Jewel confronts Marlow again: "He has left me,"

she said quietly; "you always leave us—for your own ends."
She tells Marlow that Jim "had been driven away from her
by a dream." Marlow acknowledges that all humankind,
"pushing on its blind way," is "driven by a dream of its
greatness and its power upon dark paths of excessive cruelty
and of excessive devotion."

The final witness is Gentleman Brown, interviewed on his
deathbed by Marlow. There are many ways of viewing
Brown. He, like Jones of *Victory,* together with some other
unsavory characters especially of Conrad's later period, has
been interpreted as Conrad's allegorization of the demonic.
It is true that Conrad lets Marlow speak of Brown as sailing
into Jim's history, "a blind accomplice of the Dark Powers."
He has, in Marlow's view, "a satanic gift of finding out the
best and the weakest spot in his victim." I am not persuaded,
however, that Marlow (or Conrad either) seriously enter-
tained thoughts favorable to demonology. Instead Marlow,
whom Conrad endowed with poetic gifts, seems to borrow
figurative language as served up for the occasion by a ka-
leidoscopic imagination.[16]

What is more important, I believe, than any alleged demonic sponsor of Brown is the man's psychology as Marlow
is given to understand it. For he can only guess at the motive
springs of Gentleman Brown's "cold-blooded ferocity,"
which "consoled him on his deathbed like a memory of an
indomitable defiance." Brown had balanced his account with
evil fortune by slaughtering Dain Waris and his retinue.

But, says Marlow, "It was not a vulgar and treacherous
massacre; it was a lesson, a retribution—a demonstration of
some obscure and awful attribute of our nature which, I am
afraid, is not so very far under the surface as we like to think."
In other words, I believe Marlow would say, if the "demonic"
possesses the Browns (and the Hitlers and the Khomeinis) of
the world, it threatens everyone at all times. An idealist, in
some sense as the Professor will prove to be in *The Secret
Agent,* Brown "played his part to the last." Marlow is not
sure how much Brown lied to him—"and to himself always"—but he concludes: "I did not begrudge him this

triumph *in articulo mortis,* this almost posthumous illusion of having trampled all the earth under his feet."

Jim's life ends, as already indicated, when old Doramin shoots him through the chest. Marlow tells his listeners: "They say that the white man sent right and left at all those faces a proud and unflinching glance. Then with his hand over his lips he fell forward, dead."

Marlow two years later addresses a final manuscript to the "privileged man," assuring this skeptical listener (and himself as well) that Jim had "mastered his fate" after all. Yet, at the end, Marlow sees Jim as "an obscure conqueror of fame, tearing himself out of the arms of a jealous love at the sign, at the call of his exalted egoism. He goes away from a living woman to celebrate his pitiless wedding with a shadowy ideal of conduct."

Did Conrad mean through Marlow to connect Jim's defiance of his personal fate with Brown's illusory triumph? The doubling pattern is plainly there.

"Heart of Darkness"

Since Conrad seems to have written enough of *Lord Jim* (as he thought) to insure its serialization before he began writing "Heart of Darkness" (1899), it is fair to suppose that the shorter piece represents a later conception of Marlow. The two Marlows share an identity of personality and of psychological stance—with the difference that the Marlow of "Heart of Darkness" is not as tentative in his judgment regarding Kurtz as the earlier Marlow was concerning Jim.

In "Heart of Darkness," Marlow's instinct to personal loyalty never wavers, in spite of soul-shaking moral illuminations. He is driven early to a commitment to Kurtz, moving steadily through progressive experiences of horror to his "unforeseen partnership" and in a grim kind of certitude he makes his "choice of nightmares."

The preliminary setting for the novella is similar to that of "Youth." Aboard a yawl anchored in the Thames Estuary five men, including the narrator and Marlow, again celebrate their strong "bond of the sea." Marlow is pointedly described as sitting in the "pose of a Buddha," suggesting that he has been the recipient of a weird Enlightenment, which he is impelled to share with his listeners.

Marlow begins with a meditative preamble on the conquest of the earth, recalling that England once was "one of the dark places of the earth," a land of darkness whose savagery was felt by adventurous Romans. Similarly, the conquest of a continent, "which mostly means the taking it away from those who have a different complexion or slightly flatter noses than ourselves, is not a pretty thing when you look into it too much." What redeems it, he says, is "an idea at the back of it . . . and an unselfish belief in the idea—something you can set up, and bow down before, and offer a sacrifice to. . . ." Marlow breaks off because his thoughts are upon Kurtz, a man who had "moral ideas" but who allowed his own person to become the object of worship involving human sacrifice.

Marlow's journey to Africa starts from "a whited sepulchre" of a city, presumably Brussels, where amid images of the Fates and of the Styx he obtains an appointment as captain of a steamer on a mighty river in "a place of darkness," obviously the Congo to anyone casually acquainted with Conrad's own experience with the Société Anonyme Belge pour le Commerce du Haut-Congo.

Marlow's "excellent aunt," who had helped him get the job,[17] is enthusiastic, for he will be "something like an emissary of light," helping to wean ignorant millions "from their horrid ways." Buried here is Conrad's first verbal clue as Marlow begins his journey to the core of horror. The horror is remote and external and resides, it appears, in the ways of the savages. As Marlow gets closer to his goal, the locus of horror will shift dramatically. Already Marlow is feeling like "an impostor," and it seems that, "instead of going to the centre of a continent," he is "about to set off for the centre of the earth." This and other Dantean images will accentuate the progressively grim aspect of his hell-journey.

At the same time Marlow's voyage to Africa provides a series of vivid impressions of European colonialism in the nineteenth century. The French steamer that takes him to Africa stops at every port along the African coast: "We pounded along, stopped, landed soldiers; went on, landed custom-house clerks to levy toll in what looked like a God-forsaken wilderness, with a tin shed and a flag-pole lost in it; landed more soldiers—to take care of the custom-house clerks, presumably." For Marlow the air of unreality is accentuated by the sight of "a man-of-war anchored off the coast . . . shelling the bush. . . . In the empty immensity of earth, sky, and water, there she was, incomprehensible, firing into a continent."

At the mouth of the Congo he changes to another vessel and travels upriver to the first company station, a "scene of inhabited devastation." He watches a file of men pass, each with an iron collar on his neck, all "connected together with a chain whose bights swung between them, rhythmically clinking." Marlow realizes that he also is "a part of the great cause of these high and just proceedings." From here on the deepening irony will betoken his alienation from his fellow Europeans.

Marlow walks by a vast purposeless hole being dug on a slope, then moves on past more imperialist wreckage and stumbles on "the grove of death," where some of the "helpers" had withdrawn to die: "They were not enemies, they were not criminals, they were nothing earthly now,—nothing but black shadows of disease and starvation, lying confusedly in the greenish gloom." While Marlow stands "horror-struck," one of the phantoms "rose to his hands and knees, and went off on all-fours towards the river to drink." The horror, still external, has come closer.

Marlow hurries off to the station, where he meets the company's chief accountant, whose meticulous books record that "a stream of manufactured goods, rubbishy cottons, beads, and brass-wire" was sent into "the depths of darkness, and in return came a precious trickle of ivory." From the accountant he first hears of Kurtz, a "first-class agent" in charge of a trading post "in the true ivory country."

Marlow leaves, with a safari of sixty men, to walk the two

hundred miles to the Central Station. On the way they pass abandoned villages where he notes evidence of slavers' depredations. They arrive on the fifteenth day and he learns that his river steamer will take months to repair, a delay that Marlow suspects suits the station manager who hopes that his rival Kurtz will die before Marlow can rescue him. Significantly, the manager is the first of Conrad's hollow men—"there was nothing within him."[18]

The company brickmaker, who regards Kurtz as a dangerous "emissary of pity, and science, and progress," also identifies Marlow with "the new gang—the gang of virtue." This "unforeseen partnership" is certified when the brickmaker—"this papier-mâché Mephistopheles"—is allowed to draw false inferences regarding Marlow's influence in the company. Pointedly Marlow tells his listeners that he cannot bear a lie, "not because I am straighter than the rest of us, but simply because it appalls me. There is a taint of death, a flavour of mortality in lies." But he acknowledges that he went close to a lie because he believed it "somehow would be of help" to Kurtz.

Repair work on the steamer is interrupted by the arrival of the Eldorado Exploring Expedition. And Conrad, through Marlow's fierce denunciation of the Europeans, continues his assault on the rampant imperialism that disgraced Western culture at the end of the nineteenth century. Their talk, Marlow says, "was the talk of sordid buccaneers." In words strangely appropriate for our century's tardy consciousness regarding ecological exploitation, Marlow judges the exploitation of his day: "To tear treasure out of the bowels of the land was their desire, with no more moral purpose at the back of it than there is in burglars breaking into a safe." Disgusted at the folly of the "gang" that "infested the station," Marlow gives more thought to Kurtz as a man "who had come out equipped with moral ideas of some sort."

At last the day arrives when the steamer is repaired and Marlow begins the two-month trip upriver to Kurtz's Inner Station. The subtle alienation that is progressively separating him from his fellow Europeans is complemented by the appeal of the blacks he observes along the way, and by this suspicion of their not being inhuman. . . . They howled and leaped, and spun, and made horrid faces; but what thrilled you was just the thought of their humanity—like yours—the thought of your remote kinship with this wild and passionate uproar.

Howling, leaping, making horrid faces? Here I think is Marlow's intimation of a kinship with horror, which till now had been external. Also anticipating what existentialists have called "the authentic person," Marlow feels that one "must at least be as much of a man as these on the shore. He must meet that truth with his own true stuff—with his own inborn strength."

As the steamer approaches Kurtz's station unseen natives on the riverbank attack and Marlow's helmsman is killed. The fight scene is one of Conrad's most successful passages of impressionism that at the same time attains an almost surrealistic force. Marlow is deeply moved by the death of his helmsman, and he supposes that Kurtz must have been killed also. But, as he assures his listeners, he was wrong: the privilege of meeting "the gifted Kurtz" was waiting for him. Emotion wells up afresh to interrupt Marlow's narrative, and after a long silence, Marlow blurts out: "I laid the ghost of his gifts at last with a lie."

He then gives his hearers a preview of Kurtz, describing the man's possessive mania: "Everything belonged to him. . . . The thing was to know what he belonged to." Marlow is sure that his listeners, protected by the restraints of Western civilization, cannot understand. Kurtz had gone into a wilderness that had embraced him, and he had been seduced by the "solitude without a policeman."

Marlow's listeners are told that Kurtz had been entrusted by the International Society for the Suppression of Savage Customs with the writing of a report:

It was eloquent, vibrating with eloquence, but too high-strung, I think. Seventeen pages of close writing he had found time for! But this must have been before his—let us say—nerves, went wrong, and caused him to preside at certain midnight dances ending with unspeakable rites, which—as far as I reluctantly gathered from what

I heard at various times—were offered up to him—do you understand?—to Mr. Kurtz himself.

This document, Marlow says, "was a beautiful piece of
writing," but it began ominously with the argument that "we
whites" must appear to the "savages" to be " 'supernatural
beings—we approach them with the might as of a deity,' and
so on, and so on. 'By the simple exercise of our will we can
exert a power for good practically unbounded,' etc. etc." The
document concluded with a magificent peroration, and

There were no practical hints to interrupt the magic current of
phrases, unless a kind of note at the foot of the last page, scrawled
evidently much later, in an unsteady hand, may be regarded as the
exposition of a method. It was very simple, and at the end of that
moving appeal to every altruistic sentiment it blazed at you, lu-
minous and terrifying, like a flash of lightning in a serene sky:
"Exterminate all the brutes!"

Marlow returns to his narrative and tells how he tipped
the body of his dead helmsman overboard to save his cannibal
crew members from temptation, and then steamed on to
Kurtz's station. Through his binoculars Marlow gets his first
view of the Inner Station, including the decaying headquarters
building surrounded by vestiges of a fence with its posts "or-
namented with round carved balls," which he is shocked to
learn are human heads.
    Their presence, he feels,

only showed that Mr. Kurtz lacked restraint in the gratification of
his various lusts. . . . Whether he knew of this deficiency himself I
can't say. I think the knowledge came to him at last—only at the
very last.

But, says Marlow, the wilderness

had whispered to him things about himself which he did not know,
things of which he had no conception till he took counsel with this
great solitude—and the whisper had proved irresistibly fascinating.
It echoed loudly within him because he was hollow at the core.

Thus, in anticipation, Marlow plumbs the dark depths of Kurtz's soul.

At this point, finally, Conrad gives Marlow and the readers a first view of Kurtz, borne on a stretcher and surrounded by streams of naked and armed blacks. Marlow watches as the feeble Kurtz sits up and gives commands. The blacks vanish and Kurtz is brought on board the steamboat. The manager reports to Marlow that Kurtz is very ill, and declares that it is his duty to denounce him to their superiors because his "unsound method" has done "more harm than good to the Company."

Marlow tells his listeners later, "It seemed to me I had never breathed an atmosphere so vile, and I turned mentally to Kurtz for relief." Thus in a climax of revulsion against the manager and the pilgrims, Marlow is driven to make his "choice of nightmares." His formal commitment comes quickly when he informs Kurtz's Russian disciple: "I am Mr. Kurtz's friend—in a way." And later, even though he learns that Kurtz had ordered the attack on the steamer, he further assures the Russian: "Mr. Kurtz's reputation is safe with me."

In fact, it is Marlow who rescues Kurtz from his last midnight rendezvous with his worshipers. Next day they leave the station, but not before the pilgrims fire into the crowd of natives, including a "savage and superb, wild-eyed and magnificent" creature, no doubt the mistress of Kurtz.

There is, in most editions of "Heart of Darkness," a space break after this fierce burst of irony. Marlow is made to observe:

The brown dark current ran swiftly out of the heart of darkness, bearing us down towards the sea . . . and Kurtz's life was running swiftly, too, . . . I saw the time approaching when I would be left alone of the party of "unsound method." . . . It is strange how I accepted this unforeseen partnership, this choice of nightmares forced upon me in the tenebrous land invaded by these mean and greedy phantoms.

One night Marlow comes in to find Kurtz lying "in the dark waiting for death." By the light of a candle, he sees "on that ivory face the expression of sombre pride, of ruthless power, of craven terror—of an intense and hopeless despair," and he wonders whether Kurtz lived his life again "in every detail of desire, temptation, and surrender during that supreme moment of complete knowledge." Marlow reports that Kurtz "cried in a whisper at some image, at some vision— he cried out twice, a cry that was no more than a breath—

" 'The horror! The horror!' "

Thus, with Kurtz's "final burst of sincerity," Marlow's journey to the heart of horror culminates, as vicariously he looks with Kurtz into the depths of the human soul. A short while later "the manager's boy put his insolent black head in the doorway, and said in a tone of scathing contempt—

" 'Mistah Kurtz—he dead.' "

Marlow tells his listeners that Kurtz was buried next day "and then they very nearly buried me." He survives his fever and remains "to dream the nightmare out to the end, and to show my loyalty to Kurtz once more." Also, Marlow gained some knowledge of himself.

Since I had peeped over the edge myself, I understand better the meaning of his stare, that could not see the flame of the candle, but was wide enough to embrace the whole universe, piercing enough to penetrate all the hearts that beat in the darkness. He had summed up—he had judged. "The horror!" . . . After all, this was the expression of some sort of belief; . . . And it is not my own extremity I remember best. . . . It is his extremity that I seem to have lived through.

Kurtz's cry, for Marlow, "was an affirmation, a moral victory."

Back in Europe, Marlow finds himself in "the sepulchral city" of Brussels. As custodian of Kurtz's papers, he resists prying company officials, and also an inquisitive organist who, claiming to be Kurtz's cousin, declares that his distinguished relative would have been an "immense success" as a musician. To a journalist, he gives Kurtz's document on the "Suppression of Savage Customs," but only after suppressing truth by tearing off the murderous "postscriptum."

Marlow now determines to return to Kurtz's fiancée "a

slim packet of letters and the girl's portrait." As he enters her
house amid dark and assorted symbols of death, he carries
with him a vision of Kurtz like "the heart of a conquering
darkness." He intuits that the woman has "a mature capacity
for fidelity, for belief, for suffering." By the aid of her cred-
ulous faith—and of a lie—Marlow is able to forestall this
"moment of triumph for the wilderness." When he stumbles
into an admission that he was with Kurtz to the end, "heard
his very last words," she demands to know them:

I was on the point of crying at her, "Don't you hear them?" The
dusk was repeating them in a persistent whisper all around us, . . .
"The horror! the horror!"
    "His last word—to live with," she insisted. "Don't you under-
stand I loved him—I loved him—I loved him!"
    I pulled myself together and spoke slowly.
    "The last word he pronounced was—your name."
    I heard a light sigh and then my heart stood still, stopped dead
short by an exulting and terrible cry, by the cry of inconceivable
triumph and of unspeakable pain. "I knew it—I was sure!" . . . She
knew. She was sure.

Conrad's irony has its final fillip. Marlow has long since
made it clear that he loathes a lie. Defending Kurtz against
the brickmaker, he had gone "near enough to a lie." He had
suppressed the full truth from the journalist who received
Kurtz's manuscript. Now, his defense of the woman's illusions has cost him a deliberate falsehood. But "The heavens
do not fall for such a trifle."
    So ends Marlow's communication of his dark enlighten-
ment. Conrad's narrator is left contemplating "the heart of
an immense darkness," and his readers are left to contemplate
Marlow's final "pose of a meditating Buddha"—symbol of
Conrad's fascination with illusion, emptiness, and silence.

6

Tragic Awareness—Nostromo and Mrs. Gould

Joseph Conrad was at the height of his powers when he turned to the writing of *Nostromo* (1904). He worked for two years on his ambitious design, which he told Richard Curle was "to render the spirit of an epoch in the history of South America."[1] The result was a prodigious feat of imagination, for Conrad succeeded in inventing the entire country of Costaguana—its geography and its weather, the ethnic and factional multiplicity of its people, the historical and social dynamics of a whole nation—and out of this imaginary place and time he contrived a real world of men and women "shortsighted in good and evil." Overshadowing the human activity are the mindless mountain peaks of the Cordillera and the San Tomé silver mine, symbol of the "material interests" that drive the total population of Costaguana through cycles of creativity and destructiveness.

Conrad later specifically denied that the title figure was intended to be the hero of the novel, insisting instead that "Silver is the pivot of the moral and material events, affecting the lives of everybody in the tale."[2] In view of this absence of a "hero" from *Nostromo*, I believe that a strong case can be made that the novel has a *heroine* in Mrs. Charles Gould.[3] At the same time it challenges a persistent critical notion that Conrad failed in his portrayal of feminine characters.

Nostromo

But first it is necessary to deal with Nostromo, whom Conrad explicitly demoted from the expected role of a title character. The reason, it seems to me, is that this adventurer turns out to be another of those people for whom Conrad reserved his ironic appraisal. Like Almayer and Willems, of the early Malay novels, Nostromo is made falsely aware by his idealistic conception of himself.

Gian' Battista Fidanza, called Nostromo, "our man," is a man with a reputation. Nostromo's intrepidity is certified on the day he saves the life of the liberal dictator Ribiera. "Under providence," declares Captain Mitchell, "we owed our preservation to my Capataz de Cargadores." Also saved along with the dictator of Costaguana are the company's property and the railway property, as well as the large treasure of silver ingots from the San Tomé mine. But then the Ribierist government is threatened by yet another revolution.

Into this charged situation, set with ironic mastery by Conrad, Nostromo moves with the careless intention of maintaining and extending his reputation. Regarded by Captain Mitchell as "invaluable for our work—a perfectly incorruptible fellow," he is the "indispensable man, the tried and trusty Nostromo."

There are others close to Nostromo who discern more of the character that lies behind the reputation than Captain Mitchell does. Old Teresa Viola chaffs Gian' Battista Fidanza for his acceptance of a demeaning name: "What is that? Nostromo? He would take a name that is properly no word from them."[4] Later, when Teresa is dying, she entreats Nostromo to go for her priest. He refuses, with the excuse that he is needed to save the silver of the mine. She tells him: "Then God, perhaps, will have mercy upon me! But do you look to it, man, that you get something for yourself out of it, besides the remorse that shall overtake you some day."

Don Martin Decoud, the worldly-wise and world-weary newspaperman who goes out to sea with Nostromo in the lighter loaded with silver, measures the Capataz precisely, reflecting "that this man was made incorruptible by his enormous vanity, that finest form of egoism which can take on the aspect of every virtue." When the load of silver is imperiled and with it Nostromo's reputation for competence, Decoud intuits that Nostromo resents "having been given a task in which there were so many chances of failure."

Dr. Monygham, who is the last person to see Nostromo
and Decoud when they depart on their adventure with the
silver, is the first to speak to Nostromo who returns alone.
Like the others, he sees a use for Nostromo—he persuades
the Capataz to take the message to Cayta that saves the republic. But he fails to show the interest in Nostromo that
"would have restored to him his personality." The infection
of disillusionment, begun with the taunting words of Teresa
and incubated in Nostromo's guilt at rejecting her dying request, breaks out in his bitter thoughts: "Had I not done
enough for them to be of some account *por Dios?*"

But Nostromo accepts the new assignment and makes the
epic ride to Cayta to bring General Barrios's forces by sea to
the relief of Sulaco. The death of the renegade Sotillo and the
dispersal of the Monterists complete the success of the coun-
terrevolution; and Sulaco, the Occidental Province, establishes what promises to be a flourishing independence. But
popular adulation and the acclaim of the political and social
leaders come too late to restore to Nostromo his lost self-
image. The abstraction reputation, in Nostromo's consciousness, is replaced by another abstraction, "the clear and simple
notion of betrayal." This occurs even before Nostromo receives the intelligence that Decoud is dead. Conrad suggests
the man's awakening to his lostness in language symbolic of
the Edenic fall: "Nostromo tasted the dust and ashes of the
fruit of life into which he had bitten deeply in his hunger for
praise." He feels that "his fidelity had been taken advantage
of." Conrad says: "A man betrayed is a man destroyed," an
iteration of a theme in *An Outcast of the Islands,* where he
commented on Willems's subjectivity: "Injustice destroys fidelity." Full of the sense of his "betrayed individuality," he
returns to the island-hidden treasure and there realizes that
Decoud's suicide has left the secret of the silver with him
alone.

A long passage of Conrad's blazing rhetoric ends in a picture of sunrise over the peaks of the Cordillera. The Capataz,
looking down "upon the fall of loose earth, stones, and
smashed bushes, concealing the hiding-place of the silver,"

makes his criminal choice: " 'I must grow rich very slowly,' he meditated aloud."

Mrs. Gould

If Mrs. Charles Gould is not the moving center of consciousness for Conrad in *Nostromo,* she is the novel's stable center of tragic awareness.[5] More than any other character in the novel, Emily Gould was the projection of Conrad's vision into a "twilight country" and into events "flowing from the passions of men short-sighted in good and evil."

In the first place, it is important to consider the sharp contrast Conrad set between Mrs. Gould and the novel's title character, Nostromo. Whereas "our man" with a reputation was ultimately dependent on others for his personality, Emily Gould is seen as a remarkably self-contained being. Conrad does his best to show that, despite conventions that would in that time and place trammel a woman, her small and completely feminine person is the reservoir of tremendous power. From Emily Gould flows moral energy that affects all she touches. She is the most vital character in the novel.

Conrad builds with care his portrait of this perceptive woman, who observes and experiences so much and so deeply. Through Emily Gould's speaking and acting, Conrad meant for his readers to appreciate her tenderness and her awareness. Through her sensibility he meant to convey much of what he himself had to say.

Significantly, the reader learns about the history of Costaguana precisely what Mrs. Gould knows about the country, what she tells Sir John, the railroad magnate from London, about Sulaco. She has accompanied her husband all over the province and, along with the sights, she has experienced the people's hospitality:

In all these households she could hear stories of political outrage; friends, relatives, ruined, imprisoned, killed in the battles of senseless civil wars, barbarously executed in ferocious proscriptions. . . . And on all the lips she found a weary desire for peace, the dread

of officialdom with its nightmarish parody of administration without law, without security, and without justice.

She bore a whole two months of wandering very well.

The "Never-tired Señora," as she is called by Don Pépé, is
able to appreciate "the great worth of the people," to recognize "the man under the silent, sad-eyed beast of burden."
And she observes that a peaceable Indian wearing the green
and white colors of the San Tomé mine

was somehow very seldom beaten to within an inch of his life on
a charge of disrespect to the town police; neither ran he much risk
of being suddenly lassoed on the road by a recruiting party of
lanceros—a method of voluntary enlistment looked upon as almost
legal in the Republic.

Just as Conrad manages it so that readers learn about the
land and the people of Sulaco through the mind of Mrs.
Gould, so through her consciousness are filtered insights into
the meaning of the silver mine and the establishment of the
Gould Concession. She knows the history of the San Tomé
mine. Worked in the early days by slaves, it has become at
length the object of English exploitation succeeded by gov-
ernmental expropriation and spoliation. Young Charles
Gould had fallen under the spell of the mine and, soon after
his father's death, took his bride to Costaguana. From that
time, says Conrad, the history of the mine "was in essence
the history of her married life." Mrs. Gould has seen it all
from the beginning:

She had seen the first spongy lump of silver yielded to the hazards
of the world by the dark depths of the Gould Concession; she had
laid her unmercenary hands with an eagerness that made them
tremble, upon the first silver ingot turned out still warm from the
mould; and by her imaginative estimate of its power she endowed
that lump of metal with a justificative conception.

So readers come to understand what Mrs. Gould knows
and feels about Costaguana and the San Tomé mine. Ori-

entation in these matters is paralleled by Conrad's achievement in letting Charles Gould himself develop within the ken of his wife. Emily Gould had early divined that the motivation of Charles Gould was something other than materialistic. The idea of rehabilitating the mine presented itself to the young couple as a challenge to succeed where others had failed. Conrad specifically states that "even the most legitimate touch of materialism was wanting in Mrs. Gould's character." But Charles Gould, regarding wealth only "as a means, not as an end," has explained to his wife: "I pin my faith to material interests."

Emily Gould at this stage of her development may not be able to comprehend fully Conrad's authorial pronouncement: "Action is consolatory. It is the enemy of thought and the friend of flattering illusions. Only in the conduct of our action can we find the sense of mastery over the Fates." But she does realize that the San Tomé Concession is the only field for her husband's action: "The mine had been the cause of an absurd moral disaster; its working must be made a serious and moral success."

Mrs. Gould watches as her husband's mine became "a rallying point for everything in the province that needed order and stability to live." She sees that Gould's agility is being tried by "the continuous political changes, the constant 'saving of the country,' which to her seems a puerile and bloodthirsty game of murder and rapine played with terrible earnestness by depraved children." Later, even with a measure of stability assured, rumors of violence continue to seep into the drawing room of the Casa Gould:

This gossip of the inland Campo, so characteristic of the rulers of the country with its story of oppression, inefficiency, fatuous methods, treachery, and savage brutality, was perfectly known to Mrs. Gould. That it should be accepted with no indignant comment by people of intelligence, refinement, and character as something inherent in the nature of things was one of the symptoms of degradation that had the power to exasperate her almost to the verge of despair.

Meanwhile, forced to accommodate himself to "existing circumstances of corruption," Gould refuses to discuss "the ethical view with his wife." Instead, he

trusted that, though a little disenchanted, she would be intelligent enough to understand that his character safeguarded the enterprise of their lives as much or more than his policy. The extraordinary development of the mine had put a great power into his hands. To feel that prosperity always at the mercy of unintelligent greed had grown irksome to him. To Mrs. Gould it was humiliating.

In time, with the aid of the North American financier Holroyd, "the Ribierist party in Costaguana took a practical shape under the eye of the administrator of the San Tomé mine." General Montero's military victory at Rio Seco guarantees the elevation of Don Vincente Ribiera, a doctor of philosophy from the Cordova University, as president-dictator, and the passage of a Five-Year-Mandate law that is to be the basis of Costaguana's "regeneration." At the time of Ribiera's state visit to Sulaco, "great regenerating transactions were being initiated—the fresh loan, a new railway line, a vast colonization scheme."

Mrs. Gould is the only woman present at the final luncheon for the President-Dictator. Apparently also, among those who hear Ribiera's parting speech, she is the only person to suffer any premonitory feeling. Less than six months later, "Sulaco learned with stupefaction of the military revolt in the name of national honour."

As the Monterist revolt gains momentum, Conrad's ironic vision continues to range freely over the entire country and in the minds and hearts of the principal actors of the story. Yet it is remarkable how much he continues to focus his vision on and through Mrs. Gould. No single place throughout the whole book is so often the center of action, devotion, or imagination as the Casa Gould. No other individual, not even the title figure, Nostromo, so often occupies in time and space the strategic point of awareness. In her relations with every important character in the novel, she is viewed in numerous acts "of integrity, tolerance, and compassion."

The family of old Giorgio Viola, for example, knows the English lady of Sulaco as benefactress. In the very first mention of her in the novel, the old Garibaldino reads his Italian Bible with silver-mounted spectacles presented to him by Señora Emilia Gould. It is Mrs. Gould who intervenes with Sir John and saves the Albergo d'Italia Una during the construction of the railroad. She visits Teresa in her last illness, and after her death looks after the two girls; and, finally, it is Mrs. Gould who consoles Giselle when she loses her lover.

For the people of the three mining villages, Mrs. Gould establishes schools and a hospital. It is through "the munificence of the wife of our Señor Administrador" that an altarpiece is painted in Europe for the church of Father Romàn. In fact, Mrs. Gould's concern for "these people enhanced their importance in the priest's eyes, because it really augmented his own. When talking over with her the innumerable Marias and Brigidas of the villages, he felt his own humanity expand."

As for Dr. Monygham, the company doctor, "only Mrs. Gould could keep his unbelief in men's motives within due bounds." This skeptical, bitter man is the beneficiary of Mrs. Gould's "humanizing influence." She ignores rumors that he betrayed friends during the time of Guzman Bento; and, in time, the "savage independence" of the San Tomé medical officer is "tamed" by her kindness.

Mrs. Gould keeps her old Spanish house open for the dispensation of the "small graces of existence. . . . She was highly gifted in the art of human intercourse which consists in delicate shades of self-forgetfulness and in the suggestion of universal comprehension." Conrad, with no perceptible ironic intent, devotes an entire paragraph to the line: "She was always sorry for homesick people."

Those who instinctively seek out Mrs. Gould include distinguished visitors to Sulaco like Sir John. When Holroyd and the two other tycoons from San Francisco come to talk business with Charles Gould, his wife's "unmistakable enthusiasm, pointed by a slight flavour of irony, made her talk of the mine absolutely fascinating to her visitors." The very intelligent engineer in chief, nameless throughout the novel,

always finds Mrs. Gould a responsive listener, and when the
first phase of violence reached Sulaco during the Monterist
revolt, he is impressed with her efficiency in turning the Casa
Gould into "a war hospital below, and . . . a restaurant
above." Braving the threats of rioting and other dangers, Mrs.
Gould takes Dr. Monygham in her carriage to the bedside of
the dying Teresa, and the same night drives Nostromo and
Decoud to the wharf where they depart on their mission with
the silver. Later she puts her carriage at the disposal of Antonia, who is fleeing the town with her invalid father, Don
José Avellanos.

Mrs. Gould is not restricted during the revolution to the
traditional activities of womanly mercy. Conrad provides
ample evidence that she shares the full confidence of the strat-
egists. General Pablo Barrios admires the good sense of this
woman "who did not wobble in the saddle." When shown
a petition from the bandit Hernandez, "praying the Sulaco
Assembly for permission to enlist, with all his followers, in
the forces being then raised in Sulaco for the defence of the
Five-Year Mandate of regeneration," Mrs. Gould welcomes
him and his band as allies, for she is aware of the oppressive
conditions that have driven him to outlawry.

The prime example among those who take counsel with
Mrs. Gould, apart from Charles Gould himself, is Martin
Decoud. This suave boulevardier and civilian-of-fortune has
recently completed an assignment for Don José and the Pa-
triotic Committee to arm the Sulaco troops with an improved
model of rifle that "had been just discarded for something
still more deadly by one of the great European powers." Don
Martin thinks life in Costaguana is an "opera-bouffe in which
all the comic business of stage statesmen, brigands, etc., etc.,
all their farcical stealing, intriguing, and stabbing is done in
dead earnest."

But when Decoud commits himself to the defense of Sulaco,
he comes to Mrs. Gould with his daring plan of counterrev-
olution because he thinks she is "a sensible woman." Later,
he writes his sister that Mrs. Gould is a dependable ally, and
he adds that her husband

trusts her perhaps, but I fancy rather as if he wished to make up for some subtle wrong, for that sentimental unfaithfulness which surrenders her happiness, her life, to the seduction of an idea. The little woman has discovered that he lives for the mine rather than for her. . . . Mrs. Gould's mission is to save him from the effects of that cold and overmastering passion, which she dreads more than if it were an infatuation for another woman.

That Conrad agreed with Decoud's view of the relationship between Charles and Emily Gould is confirmed, more than a hundred pages later, when the omniscient author analyzes the "subtle conjugal infidelity through which his wife was no longer the sole mistress of his thoughts."

When Charles Gould determines to dynamite the mine rather than surrender it, he returns to the Casa Gould. His wife senses an ominous turn of affairs: " 'Why don't you tell me something?' she almost wailed." Gould tells her only that he is returning to the mine to bring down the silver, and as he bends to kiss her she disengages her hand from his "to smooth his cheek with a light touch, as if he were a little boy."

At the same time, Conrad's juxtaposition of another symbol, the serpent in Paradise, suggests that his Adam and Eve are experiencing a subtle alienation from one another. Charles Gould's failure to reveal to his wife his whole grim intention is, in the face of her earnest request for information, a sign of his lack of faith.

Significantly, this act of distrust is followed almost immediately by the entry of Martin Decoud, who provides a devastating analysis of Gould, accelerating the disenchantment of Gould's wife. Decoud, as tempter, proposes to Mrs. Gould that the rumor of Montero's victory and the defeat of the Ribierists be suppressed so that the large silver load may be allowed to come down the mountain. Thus it comes about that Emily Gould conceals the truth from her husband "for the first and last time of her life."

The subtle attrition upon the relationship of the Goulds continues as the revolution progresses. With Decoud missing

and presumed lost along with Nostromo and the silver,
Charles Gould retires further into his own thoughts. Mrs.
Gould watches her husband with dread, and at the same time
she thinks of Antonia's loss of Decoud:

"What would I have done if Charley had been drowned while
we were engaged?" she exclaimed, mentally, with horror. . . . The
tears burst out of her eyes.
"Antonia will kill herself!" she cried out.

Here the omniscient author permits himself a rare instance
of irony at Mrs. Gould's expense. Dr. Monygham, who feels
"tender admiration" for Doña Emilia, hears her outcry:

"She thinks of that girl," he said to himself; "she thinks of the
Viola children; she thinks of me; of the wounded; of the miners;
she always thinks of everybody who is poor and miserable! . . . No
one seems to be thinking of her."

Conrad has made it clear that Emily Gould, like Gerard Man-
ley Hopkins's Margaret, is mourning for herself.

It is part of Conrad's master plan of irony that Dr. Monygham, whose love for Emily Gould is "like an enlightening
and priceless misfortune," replaces Decoud as her cynical
tutor. Years after the revolution and the establishment of
Sulaco's flourishing independence, the Goulds return from an
extended stay abroad, and are met by Dr. Monygham. Gould
goes at once to tend to the silver mine, and Mrs. Gould invites
the doctor to lunch. Monygham feels a "pitying emotion at
the marks of time upon the face of that woman, the air of
frailty and weary fatigue that had settled upon the eyes and
temples of the 'Never-tired Señora.' " He informs Mrs. Gould
that her friends, Antonia Avellanos and the Cardinal-
Archbishop Corbelàn, together with political refugees from
Sta. Marta, are conspiring for the invasion of Costaguana:

"Will there be never any peace? Will there be no rest?" Mrs.
Gould whispered. "I thought that we—"
"No!" interrupted the doctor. "There is no peace and no rest in

the development of material interests. . . . Mrs. Gould, the time approaches when all that the Gould Concession stands for shall weigh as heavily upon the people as the barbarism, cruelty, and misrule of a few years back."

Monygham continues his brutal lesson, and she asks hopelessly, "Is it this we have worked for, then?" When Dr. Monygham leaves her, Mrs. Gould leans back in her garden seat, her eyes closed and her hands lying idle:

Small and dainty, as if radiating a light of her own in the deep shade of the interlaced boughs, she resembled a good fairy, weary with a long career of well-doing, touched by the withering suspicion of the uselessness of her labours, the powerlessness of her magic.

This is the intensest moment of tragic illumination in the book. In her loneliness, she thinks of her "incorrigible" husband—

Incorrigible in his hard, determined service of the material interests to which he had pinned his faith in the triumph of order and justice. . . . There was something inherent in the necessities of successful action which carried with it the moral degradation of the idea. She saw the San Tomé mountain hanging over the Campo, over the whole land, feared, hated, wealthy; more soulless than any tyrant, more pitiless and autocratic than the worst Government; ready to crush innumerable lives in the expansion of its greatness. He did not see it. He could not see it. It was not his fault. He was perfect, perfect; but she would never have him to herself.

For Emily Gould the circle of tragic awareness is closed. Years before, Charles Gould had told his wife that the great silver and iron interests would some day "get hold of Costaguana along with the rest of the world." She had protested at this "most awful materialism," and Gould had said, "My dear, it's nothing to me. . . . I make use of what I see." The material interests, she now understands, have used her husband. In her loneliness she is reminded of her childlessness, and "an immense desolation, the dread of her own continued life, descended upon the first lady of Sulaco. With a prophetic vision she saw herself surviving alone the degradation of her young ideal of life, of love, of work—all alone in the Treasure House of the World."

There remains, in the novel, the logical working out of Emily Gould's tragic awareness as it touches her relationship with the title figure, Nostromo. When Dr. Monygham gives her a report on the tangled affairs of the Viola girls and their lovers, she reacts uneasily, feeling her "duty toward these girls." She takes seriously her role as "the providence of the Viola family," but Conrad, employing gentle irony, suggests that hers is a limited providence: " 'A word will be enough for a man like Nostromo. . . . He must put an end to all this by marrying Linda at once,' pronounced the first lady of Sulaco with immense decision."

Mrs. Gould never has a chance to speak to Nostromo about Linda, for he is cut down by the rifle of old Giorgio Viola. The dying man sends for her and confesses his theft of the lost load of silver. His words overwhelm her with the sense of the triviality of the treasure:

The silver has killed me. It has held me. It holds me yet. Nobody knows where it is. But you are the wife of Don Car os, who put it into my hands and said, "Save it on your life." And when I returned, and you all thought it was lost, what do I hear? "It was nothing of importance. Let it go. Up, Nostromo, the faithful, and ride away to save us, for dear life!"

She whispers in reply: "I, too, have hated the idea of that silver from the bottom of my heart." She refuses to let Nostromo tell her where the silver is hidden: "No one misses it now. Let it be lost forever."

Dr. Monygham is waiting for her outside:

" 'Now, Mrs. Gould,' he said almost brutally in his impatience, 'tell me, was I right? There is a mystery. You have got the word of it, have you not? He told you—' "

And Mrs. Gould, who once suppressed the truth from her husband concerning this same silver, manages now a deliberate lie: " 'He told me nothing,' said Mrs. Gould, steadily."[6]

Then, while she waits for her carriage, she comforts Giselle.

Conrad says that, feeling the girl's suppressed sobbing, she "had the first and only moment of bitterness in her life":

> "Console yourself, child. Very soon he would have forgotten you for his treasure."
> "Señora, he loved me. . . ."
> "I have been loved, too," Mrs. Gould said in a severe tone.

The last view of Mrs. Gould is symbolic. She, who has learned that she cannot do everything, asks Dr. Monygham about Nostromo's condition: "You can do nothing?" And the doctor replies: "No, Mrs. Gould. . . . Useless."

So we find Mrs. Gould, one of Conrad's most intelligent characters, at the end of one of his most pessimistic books— a work in which ideals and events are subverted by faithlessness and futility. Nostromo, with its vision of the uselessness of private dreams and of public activity even when motivated by decent impulses, remains a remarkable index to human nature and at the same time a chastening testament of futility to a world that since the publication of the novel in 1904 has so often seen its hopes subverted by violence.

7

The Secret Agent

For *The Secret Agent* (1907), regarded by some as the first modern spy novel, Joseph Conrad devised a melodramatic plot based on an actual terrorist conspiracy to blow up the Royal Greenwich Observatory. He then loaded his melodrama with heavily ironic elements of international intrigue and domestic tragedy, peopling the London of his book with an astonishing spectrum of personalities.

Daniel R. Schwarz has argued cogently that the major character of *The Secret Agent* is the narrator, who attacks a world he despises.[1] I have no problem with this judgment so long as this narrative voice is seen essentially as a projection of Conrad's fierce feelings against his own world of insanity, stupidity, and hypocrisy. In his author's note Conrad said that his artistic purpose "was formulated with deliberation and in the earnest belief that ironic treatment alone would enable me to say all I felt I would have to say in scorn as well as in pity."

At the same time, Conrad stressed that the novel was "Mrs. Verloc's story." The secret agent's wife, he said, had a "tragic suspicion" that "life doesn't stand much looking into." This statement might seem to suggest that Winnie Verloc is endowed with a fully tragic sense of life, that she belongs among those who are aware beyond their moral ability. In the text itself, however, she is limited to something less than an intellectual understanding of herself and her world.

The figures grouped around Mrs. Verloc, including her husband, her mother, her slow-witted brother, and assorted anarchists, embassy officials, police officers, and aristocrats, manifest many kinds and degrees of false or faulty awareness. With the exception of Winnie Verloc, whom Conrad regarded with a remote kind of compassion, all the people in the book are treated with a fiercely comic intention to prove that "perverse unreason has its own logical processes."

The opening chapter of *The Secret Agent* introduces Adolph Verloc, master of a sordid Soho ménage in the London of the 1880s. From this combination house and shop are purveyed a pornographic inventory of items brought from Paris by Mr. Verloc. Actually, the shop, which also displays radical political tracts, is a front for Verloc's real vocation as a secret agent in the employ of the "Embassy of a Great Power," presumably czarist Russia. Verloc has been assigned by the Embassy to infiltrate the various socialist and anarchist groups inhabiting London. But, aware that the English authorities are watching him and his shop, he buys immunity by trading information to the London police.

The double agent's domestic complacency is shattered by a summons to the embassy, where Mr. Vladimir reprehends him for his ineffectualness as an agent provocateur. Vladimir orders a dynamite outrage against the Greenwich Observatory.

Conrad now provides an interlude in which his readers meet a wretched assortment of revolutionaries and anarchists gathered at the Verloc quarters in Brett Street, Soho. There is Michaelis, obese idealist and ex-convict; he now enjoys the patronage of the aristocratic Lady Mabel, who has provided him with a cottage in the country where he is writing a book. There is Karl Yundt, worn-out "veteran of dynamite wars" who still evokes "sinister impulses which lurk in the blind envy and exasperated vanity of ignorance, in the suffering and misery of poverty, in all the hopeful and noble illusions of righteous anger, pity, and revolt." And there is Comrade Ossipon, a muscular young man, ex-medical student, and author of cheap pamphlets that have attracted the notice of the police.

Such are the types Conrad sets forth. Reduced by his withering sarcasm to caricatures, they yet contain a symbolic essence distilled from childhood memories of futile Polish revolutionaries and, presumably, from accurate knowledge of underground activity in contemporary London.[2]

Present elsewhere in the house during the gathering is Winnie's feeble-minded brother. The "innocent Stevie" is presented as a parody of simple idealism outraged by visions of cruelty and pain.[3] Here and elsewhere in the novel Stevie's explosive responses foreshadow Winnie Verloc's own violent reaction when she comes to experience her husband's betrayal. Conrad places his ironic cachet on this chapter by having Winnie ask her husband, "Shall I put out the light now?" And Verloc answers, "Yes. Put it out."

The next thing the reader learns is that the Greenwich Park bombing has taken place, and an unknown perpetrator has died in what was undoubtedly a premature blast. Another anarchist, the monomaniac Professor, tells Ossipon that he has constructed an explosive device for Adolph Verloc. Both conclude that the unidentified victim of the attempt to blow up the Greenwich Observatory was the secret agent himself. Ossipon, a robust parasite on women, finds himself contemplating "Mrs. Verloc's bereaved person and business." The Professor himself roams the streets and alleys of a London that in its mingled decay and vitality is reminiscent of the London of Charles Dickens.[4] The author's sardonic comments on this perfect anarchist demonstrate Conrad's profound insight into the psychosocial springs of terrorist activity.

In a London alley the perfect anarchist encounters the almost perfect policeman, Chief Inspector Heat of the Special Crime Department. For, although Conrad makes clear his respect for this stalwart official, he nevertheless deems Chief Inspector Heat to be "not very wise—at least not truly so." This instance of counterpoint is matched by further evidence of Conrad's skillful plotting: Heat is placed in a situation that neatly doubles Vladimir's summoning of Verloc to the embassy. The Chief Inspector is called on the carpet by the Assistant Commissioner, for Heat had only recently assured his superior that London's anarchist colony was effectively neutralized. Now the Greenwich Park atrocity has shattered *his* complacency.

Furthermore, the conflicting judgments and secret motivations of the Chief Inspector and the Assistant Commissioner are, in Conrad's steady ironic vision, seen to mirror the shabby thoughts and actions of the criminal classes. Since the Chief Inspector enjoys a useful working relationship with the secret agent Verloc, he intends to protect Verloc from implication in the Greenwich bombing. In Heat's view, the despised Michaelis is a likely scapegoat with which to appease public anger over the observatory outrage. But Heat's intention is frustrated by his superior, the Assistant Commissioner, who has his private reasons for protecting Michaelis from arrest.

When the Assistant Commissioner presses Heat to give up his privately collected evidence in the bombing case, Heat acknowledges that when he was called to the morgue to view the bomb victim's mangled remains, he had retrieved a scrap of cloth containing the Brett Street address of his prize informer, Adolph Verloc. Thus the Assistant Commissioner is startled to learn for the first time that his subordinate has been making use of a spy in the pay of a foreign government. The Assistant Commissioner decides to circumvent Heat, and to deal with Verloc himself; chapter 7 ends as he is on the way to the Soho residence/shop of the secret agent.

Conrad now—almost at midpoint in the novel—has concluded his remorseless census-taking of London's inhabitants on all sides of the law. His ironic exposition of intrigue is proceeding at embassy level and in the streets of London, in the police department and in even the halls of Westminster. It remains for him to elaborate the multiple deceptions that subvert the Verloc household. In a celebrated chapter, he recounts, by flashback, the dreary cab ride of Winnie Verloc's mother to a charity home for the aged. He details the humble intrigue of the mother who remembers how Winnie sacrificed more romantic prospects in order to accept Verloc's offer of more promising security for her mother and her slow-witted brother. The ailing mother's voluntary removal from the Verloc household, an act of "heroism and unscrupulousness," Conrad says, was based on "the cold and reasonable view that the less strain put on Mr. Verloc's kindness the longer its effects were likely to last." Thus she confirms her daughter's secret bargain with fate seven years before.

In a scene involving a maimed cab driver and his infirm horse, Conrad once again illustrates Stevie's outraged idealism in the presence of suffering. The retarded youth's actions parody the concept of tragic awareness: "Supremely wise in knowing his own powerlessness, Stevie was not wise enough to restrain his passions." Although Winnie Verloc sympathizes with her brother's raging compassion, her placid nature is balanced by her prudent notion that "it may be good for one not to know too much."

Winnie is, however, permitted a limited access to certain unpleasant aspects of the truth. To Stevie's confused suggestion that the police could help poor horses and poor cabbies, Winnie replies: "Don't you know what the police are for, Stevie? They are there so that them as have nothing shouldn't take anything away from them who have."

The chapter ends with the Verlocs in a classic scene of domestic alienation, and for a second time Conrad indulges in a heavily ironic allusion to Shakespeare's *Othello:* Winnie asks:

"Shall I put the light out?"
Mr. Verloc snapped at his wife huskily, "Put it out."

Chapter 9 opens with Verloc's return from the Continent, and a few days later his wife agrees to Verloc's suggestion that her brother be allowed to visit Michaelis. Conrad remarks casually that Winnie Verloc, therefore, "was alone longer than usual on the day of the attempted bomb outrage in Greenwich Park, because Mr. Verloc went out very early that morning and did not come back till nearly dusk." And the reader in this way learns that the secret agent was not the victim of the explosion near the observatory.

Verloc denies that he has been to see Stevie. Instead he tells Winnie that he has taken all their money out of the bank, and he talks of emigrating to France or California. They are interrupted by the arrival of a visitor, a stranger to Winnie, but the reader realizes that Conrad has spliced the plot back to chapter 7. The Assistant Commissioner takes Verloc away; and, almost immediately, the shop bell rings and Winnie admits another stranger, who introduces himself as Chief Inspector Heat of the Special Crimes Section. Heat quickly infers that his superior has beaten him to Verloc, but he produces the scrap of overcoat and its label with the Brett Street address. The bewildered Winnie recognizes it—"That's my brother's, then." Heat quizzes her with merciless politeness. Winnie's dazed response confirms Heat's conclusion that her husband and her brother were the two suspects observed by witnesses in the Greenwich Park area.

At this moment Verloc returns, alone, to be confronted by Heat. The grief-crazed Winnie hears enough of their dialogue to understand how her husband has used and destroyed Stevie. The Chief Inspector, considering the threat of a public revelation of the facts in the case, urges the secret agent to flee. Heat departs from the novel, an interesting forerunner of the principals in the Watergate and Iran-Contra affairs who carried on extralegal maneuvers in the name of national security.

But Conrad is not finished with Heat's superior. The Assistant Commissioner first reports to Westminster on the solution to the observatory outrage, only to find that Sir Ethelred, preoccupied with parliamentary feuding at high levels, is not interested in a "domestic drama." He then joins his wife at the house of "the great lady patroness of Michaelis," pleased to report to Lady Mabel that her favorite ex-convict has been cleared of complicity in the bombing plot.

Unexpectedly, the Assistant Commissioner meets there with Vladimir, the first secretary of the embassy, and in an ironic and oblique exchange he makes Vladimir understand that the bomb plot's aim to shock England into repressive measures has failed: " 'We can put our finger on every anarchist here,' went on the Assistant Commissioner. . . . 'All that's wanted now is to do away with the agent provocateur to make everything safe.' " Conrad, however, has arranged it so that Winnie Verloc and not the authorities will do away with the agent provocateur. The complicated choreography of the entire novel has been moving to a melodramatic and macabre pas de deux danced out by husband and wife.

Conrad later declared in his author's note that the novel was the story of Winnie Verloc "from the days of her childhood to the end." Acknowledging that the book was "suggested and centred round the absurd cruelty" of an actual Greenwich Park explosion, he nevertheless viewed Verloc and the other characters as "figures grouped about Mrs. Verloc." Certainly Conrad, in the final pages of the novel shifts the reader's attention away from the secret agent, who "imagined himself loved by that woman."

Unable to comprehend the value of Stevie in his wife's eyes, Verloc is unaware of her thoughts, which Conrad brilliantly transmits on pages reviewing Winnie's years of protective care and sacrifice on behalf of Stevie. As Verloc harangues his wife, Conrad informs his readers what Winnie is thinking:

> Every nook and cranny of her brain was filled with the thought that this man . . . took the boy away to kill him! . . . And across that thought . . . the form of Mr. Verloc went to and fro, . . . stamping with his boots upon her brain. He was probably talking, too; but Mrs. Verloc's thought for the most part covered the voice.

Winnie is beginning to perceive that with Stevie dead, she is a "free woman." She dresses to leave, but Verloc stops her and, says Conrad, "Mrs. Verloc's disconnected wits went to work practically."

The murder scene is masterfully realized. Verloc, reclining on the sofa, growls huskily:

> "I wish to goodness . . . I had never seen Greenwich Park or anything belonging to it."
> The veiled sound filled the small room with its moderate volume, well adapted to the modest nature of the wish. The waves of air of the proper length, propagated in accordance with correct mathematical formulas, flowed around all the inanimate things in the room, lapped against Mrs. Verloc's head as if it had been a head of stone. . . . Greenwich Park. A park! That's where the boy was killed. A park—smashed branches, torn leaves, gravel, bits of broth-

erly flesh and bone, all spouting up together in the manner of a firework. She remembered now what she had heard, and she remembered it pictorially.... Mrs. Verloc closed her eyes desperately, throwing upon that vision the night of her eyelids, where after a rainlike fall of mangled limbs the decapitated head of Stevie lingered suspended alone, and fading out slowly like the last star of a pyrotechnic display. Mrs. Verloc opened her eyes.

Conrad reports: "Her face was no longer stony.... Her wits, no longer disconnected, were working under the control of her will."

Verloc, reclining full length on the sofa, calls to Winnie:

" 'Come here,' he said in a peculiar tone, which might have been the tone of brutality, but was intimately known to Mrs. Verloc as the note of wooing."

Winnie starts forward at once

as if she were still a loyal woman bound to the man by an unbroken contract. Her right hand skimmed slightly the end of the table, and when she had passed on towards the sofa the carving knife had vanished without the slightest sound from the side of the dish.... He saw partly on the ceiling and partly on the wall the moving shadow of an arm with a clenched hand holding a carving knife. It flickered up and down. Its movements were leisurely....

But they were not leisurely enough to allow Mr. Verloc the time to move either hand or foot.... Into that plunging blow, delivered over the side of the couch, Mrs. Verloc had put all the inheritance of her immemorial and obscure descent, the simple ferocity of the age of caverns, and the unbalanced nervous fury of the age of barrooms. Mr. Verloc, the Secret Agent, turning slightly on his side with the force of the blow, expired without stirring a limb, in the muttered sound of the word "Don't" by way of protest.

As noted earlier, Conrad remembered this novel as the story of Winnie Verloc—he believed that he had told her story from the days of her childhood to "its anarchistic end of utter desolation, madness and despair." Her end is recounted in a very few pages and, ultimately, offstage. After the crime that frees her "with a perfection of freedom which left her nothing to desire and absolutely nothing to do," Winnie rushes in headlong flight from the house.

In the fog she meets with Ossipon and a grotesque comedy of errors takes place. For the anarchist, following the Professor's advice, is on his way to the Soho shop to comfort the widow, as he supposes, of the bombing accident in Greenwich Park. Winnie leads him back to the house, where he is stunned to discover Verloc's body. Winnie importunes him: "Don't let them hang me, Tom! Take me out of the country." When Ossipon realizes she has Verloc's money, he agrees to accompany her on the boattrain to France. But when the train is in motion, he leaps off with the money. A few days later Ossipon reads a news account of the suicide of a woman passenger on the Channel boat. Shaken by the "cursed knowledge" of his complicity in Winnie's death, he sits in a pub listening to the mad monologue of the Professor.

The book ends as the two men part, Ossipon "marching in the gutter" with the embassy's "secret-service money (inherited from Mr. Verloc) in his pockets." And the incorruptible Professor "walked frail, insignificant, shabby, miserable—and terrible in the simplicity of his idea calling madness and despair to the regeneration of the world."

In the opening pages of this book, Conrad, adopting what was for him a rare tone of personal engagement with his readers, remarked that the secret agent had about him an air "common to men who live on the vices, the follies, or the baser fears of mankind; the air of moral nihilism." And, also early in the book, he recorded that Mr. Verloc "descended into the abyss of moral reflections." Thoughtful readers, putting down the book, realize that Conrad has carried them into the abyss, where he has made them to breathe the fumes of moral nihilism.

8

Under Western Eyes

Under Western Eyes (1911), structurally one of Conrad's most complicated works, is the last of his great political novels (after *Nostromo* and *The Secret Agent*). Set in the sinister landscape of czarist autocracy, it is the story of a university student named Razumov—indeed, the original manuscript title was "Razumov." In the author's note (1920), written after the overthrow of the old regime and the establishment of an equally detested despotism, Conrad denied "special experience" and claimed only "general knowledge of the condition of Russia and of the moral and emotional reactions of the Russian temperament to the pressure of tyrannical lawlessness, which, in general human terms, could be reduced to the formula of senseless desperation provoked by senseless tyranny."

Well aware of his deep bias against all things Russian, Conrad acknowledged his anxious desire in writing the novel to maintain "scrupulous impartiality." He declared that he never before had been called to a greater effort of "detachment from all passions, prejudices and even from personal memories."

Conrad's strategy for preserving "detachment" in this novel was derived from the success he had had with Marlow as a narrative device. To tell Razumov's story he created an elderly Englishman, an unnamed teacher of languages residing in Geneva, who has access to pertinent documents and who (like Marlow) is at times an observer/participant. This mildly eccentric Englishman, in telling his "Russian story for Western ears," provides Conrad with the means of projecting his own prejudices as well as his insights. On the very first page of the novel, the teacher is made to express a characteristic Conradian notion: "Words, as is well known, are the great foes of reality."

Part 1, comprising about a fourth of the book's length, is a fairly straightforward account by the language teacher, based largely on Razumov's journal, the young student's record of events in St. Petersburg that would eventually send him to join the Russian colony in Geneva. Razumov is the illegitimate son of a nobleman, Prince K———, who while refusing to acknowledge his son publicly, has been sending him money privately.

Disaster invades the tranquil academic life of Razumov as a consequence of the assassination of a high government official.[1] He is astounded to learn that the assassin is a student acquaintance named Haldin. His dismay turns to dread when Haldin seeks his help in escaping. He agrees to take a message to Ziemianitch who will drive Haldin to safety. But he finds the sleigh driver dead drunk, and after trying vainly to beat the man awake he leaves, convinced that his involvement with the conspirators has doomed him. As he walks back in the snow, feeling rage at the threat to his self-preservation and despair at having no family or friends, he discovers "what he had meant to do all along." He mutters, "I shall give him up." The young man, whose name in Russian suggests "son of reason," rationalizes:

What is betrayal? . . . There must be a moral bond first. All a man can betray is his conscience. And how is my conscience engaged here; by what bond of common faith, of common conviction, am I obliged to let that fanatical idiot drag me down with him?

Instead of informing the police, Razumov goes to the palace of the prince, who takes him to General T———. There he denounces Haldin, and arrangements are made to arrest the young terrorist without implicating Razumov. Haldin departs, as he supposes, for a rendezvous with Ziemianitch and flight to safety. Razumov sits in his room knowing that Haldin is on his way to arrest and execution.

Part 1 of the novel ends with the celebrated scene of confrontation between Razumov and Councillor Mikulin. Summoned to the general secretariat, Razumov endures a tense meeting with the bureaucrat, who first informs him of Haldin's grim fate. As the interview proceeds, Mikulin probes and Razumov parries until at last he claims the right "to be done once for all" with Haldin. He asks permission to leave, and moves toward the door, thinking,

"Now he must show his hand. He must ring and have me arrested before I am out of the building, or he must let me go. And either way . . ."
An unhurried voice said—
"Kirylo Sidorovitch."
Razumov at the door turned his head.
"To retire," he repeated.
"Where to?" asked Councillor Mikulin softly.

Parts 2 and 3, comprising the middle half of the novel, shift to a time and place within the scope of the language teacher's direct observation. A long-time resident of Switzerland, he has enjoyed the acquaintance of two members of the Russian colony in Geneva—a Mrs. Haldin and her daughter Natalia. The daughter, in her own student days, had been "suspected of holding independent views on matters settled by official teaching," and both women were suspected of "liberalism." When news arrives of the arrest of Victor Haldin as a terrorist assassin, the Haldins are convinced that their son and brother was betrayed. Some weeks later, at the Chateau Borel, Natalia meets Razumov, who has been accepted by the Geneva crowd as a bona fide conspirator and revolutionist—presumed to be the escaped accomplice of Victor Haldin.

Conrad fills pages with heavy irony as Natalia seeks information and consolation from her brother's trusted friend, and Razumov struggles to defend himself against her innocent probing of his guilty conscience. And the language teacher, still ignorant of Razumov's part in betraying Haldin, presses the wary man for an explanation of Haldin's arrest and subsequent execution. At the end of their talk, the professor leaves Razumov hanging over the parapet of a bridge over the Rhone River; and here, at the beginning of Part 3, the point of view wavers noticeably as Conrad takes over the mind of Razumov.

The young double agent continues to be regarded, as the conspirator Peter Ivanovitch tells him, as "one of us—*un des notres.*"[2] Although he experiences a progressive revulsion from the inhabitants of the Chateau Borel, he doggedly pursues his goal of winning the trust of Sophia Antonovna, a particularly dangerous adversary, and the other revolutionaries. Avoiding explicit lies, he manages to satisfy their curiosity and his conscience by some deft double-talk.

When word comes from St. Petersburg that Ziemianitch has committed suicide, the conspirators conclude that it was the sledgedriver who betrayed Haldin. Razumov realizes that although they have come close to the truth, an incredible chance has delivered him.

Part 3 ends as Razumov crosses to the Ile Rousseau where, sitting beneath a bronze effigy of the revolutionary philosopher, he begins to fill the pages of a notebook; and he thinks: "There can be no doubt that now I am safe."

Part 4 opens with a self-conscious statement by the old language teacher, a mannered device by which Conrad connects the final section of the book with its first section. The reader learns that Councillor Mikulin's sardonic query "Where to?" has triggered further conversation. Mikulin had assured Razumov: "God alone knows the future. . . . But I may have occasion to require you again. . . . You have been already the instrument of Providence." Here Conrad works a favorite metaphor for all the irony it is worth. As Razumov agonizes over his Judas-like complicity in Haldin's death, he rationalizes: "I might have been the chosen instrument of Providence." But he sits "like a man totally abandoned by Providence—desolate."

A few weeks later he is summoned to the first of a series of secret interviews with Mikulin, and the story pauses while the author speaks through the thoughts of the language teacher, offering a characteristic Conradian appraisal of "mere mortal man, with his many passions and his miserable ingenuity in error, always dazzled by the base glitter of mixed motives, everlastingly betrayed by a short-sighted wisdom."

The professor is allowed to proceed with an analysis of the intricacies of bureaucratic personality—and the perilous limits of bureaucratic power. Councillor Mikulin, though fated himself to suffer ultimate downfall, receives a promotion to direct the Russian police network throughout Europe, and he thinks again of Razumov and proposes for him a dangerous assignment: to penetrate the revolutionary circle in Geneva. Razumov agrees to take on the assignment and the reader is brought back to the young double agent, sitting under Rousseau's bronze statue, composing his first report for his imperial employees.

The language teacher, again an observer/participant in the story, accompanies Natalia Haldin to the Chateau Borel, where she and Razumov meet again. The language professor, who is a forgotten bystander, intuits the powerful attraction the two young people have for each other, but he is unprepared for the sudden turn of their conversation. Razumov hints that the real betrayer of her brother was someone other than Ziemianitch and to the dazed sister he describes himself. Bewildered at first, she then "with a sort of despairing insight" receives his "atrocious confession."

Later Razumov completes his secret journal, in which he tells Natalia:

You were appointed to undo the evil by making me betray myself back into truth and peace. . . . And you have done it in the same way, too, in which he ruined me: by forcing upon me your confidence.

Razumov makes an even uglier admission—that he had once determined that the way to avenge himself on Haldin would be to "steal his sister's soul from her."[3]

After sending his journal to Natalia, he seeks out the revolutionists and repeats to them his confession. Nikita the executioner punishes him by deafening him with powerful blows to the head, and shortly thereafter Razumov walks into the path of a streetcar and suffers broken limbs and a crushed chest. Tekla, faithful *dame de compagnie* in the anarchist camp, follows him to the hospital and later nurses the cripple back to a semblance of health.

In typical fashion, Conrad concludes the novel in a series of anticlimactic ironies.

The language teacher, after two years, meets Sophia Antonovna and learns that Natalia Haldin has returned to Russia, where she is "sharing her compassionate labours between the horrors of overcrowded jails, and the heartrending misery of bereaved homes." Sophia Antonovna has also seen Razumov, who is still being cared for by the devoted Tekla. She remarks: "Some of *us* always go to see him when passing through. He is intelligent. He has ideas. . . . He talks well, too."

She then tells the professor that Nikita has "turned out to be a scoundrel of the worst kind—a traitor himself, a betrayer—a spy!" Councillor Mikulin, before his own downfall, had deliberately exposed the sinister Nikita in a chance conversation with Peter Ivanovitch.[4] Sophia Antonovna adds a final word on the Arch-Revolutionist himself: "Peter Ivanovitch is an inspired man."

Thus Conrad ends his tale of betrayal and counterbetrayal on a grimly comic note with one revolutionary commenting admiringly on the unflagging zeal of another.

9

"The Secret Sharer"

"The Secret Sharer" (1910) is a critic's dream of a story, frequently anthologized and universally admired for its tantalizing psychological clues and its symbolic richness. I include a discussion of this short work chiefly because of its thematic connection with *Under Western Eyes*. In that novel, Razumov gave the criminal Haldin up to the authorities—and as a consequence suffered for the betrayal of a fated and unwelcome partnership. In "The Secret Sharer," the unnamed captain/narrator is loyal to his secret double, defying all the formal structures of a lawful society to help an accused criminal escape.[1]

Still another parallel arises between the narrator's relation to his secret sharer and the subtle identification Captain Marlow felt with Jim, another young officer who violated the code of the sea. Indeed, one wonders whether the unnamed narrator of "The Secret Sharer" is not the same Marlow whose first "command" was a lifeboat with a crew of two, in *Youth,* and whose harrowing journey into the heart of darkness resulted in an "unforeseen partnership" with the criminal Kurtz.

This unnamed captain, reflecting on an experience of years past, tells his readers of his first real command—when he was appointed to take a ship home to England, when the crisis of initiation into knowledge of his ship and his crew was complicated by an unforeseen partnership with an escaped criminal. This "episode from the coast," the narrator recalls, occurred in the Gulf of Siam, just off Cambodia.

As the sailing ship awaits a favorable wind, darkness falls, and the captain surprises the crew by taking the anchorwatch himself. As he strolls the silent deck in his sleeping-suit, his serene reverie is broken by his discovery that the rope side-ladder has not been hauled in. The captain is astonished to find that a naked swimmer is floating at the end of the ladder. In the quiet of the sleeping ship, the two talk and the man, named Leggatt, elects to come on board. The captain, sensing "a mysterious communication" has been established between them, provides his intuitively perceived "double" with an identical sleeping-suit.

As the dialogue continues, the captain is startled to learn that Leggatt, a young chief mate, has killed a man at sea and has been held prisoner for weeks aboard the *Sephora*. As Leggatt relates the particulars of the homicide, the captain finds that the fugitive appeals to him "as if our experiences had been identical as our clothes." Leggatt tells how a seaman panicked during the fury of a storm as they were trying to set a reefed foresail, how he fought the man—and later, when the storm subsided, the seaman was dead and Leggatt was charged with his murder. As the captain listens to the account, his identification with Leggatt deepens: "I saw it all going on as though I were myself inside that other sleeping-suit." He takes Leggatt to his stateroom, and the grimly comic game of hosting his "secret sharer" begins.

Part 2 of the tale opens with a visit from Captain Archbold, skipper of the *Sephora,* who is searching for his fugitive first officer. The narrator later will state that "I could not, I think, have met him by a direct lie"—and "for psychological (not moral) reasons." But, in a manner reminiscent of the Marlow of "Heart of Darkness," the unnamed narrator does go beyond deceptive actions to protect his partner with saving lies. Conrad works, as in the earlier story, to set an ironic contrast between the individual outlaw and the forces that dominate society. Although Captain Archbold admits that Leggatt's reefed sail saved his ship in the storm, this self-righteous guardian of law and order is determined to give his mate up to the shore authorities. Leggatt's protector goes through the successful charade of showing his suspicious visitor over the ship, and at last Archbold leaves empty-handed.

The ship makes its way down the east side of the Gulf of

Siam and at last, among some islands off Cambodia, the captain agrees to help Leggatt swim to freedom. To the surprise of the crew, the captain tacks the ship and sails in dangerously close to shore. He smuggles Leggatt into the saillocker, and just before they shake hands and part, he places his protective hat on his "other self."

By now the crewmen are watching in awed silence as the ship moves toward the towering blackness of Koh-ring. The captain, a stranger to his ship, finds it impossible to tell whether she is moving safely away from disaster until in the gathering darkness he detects, floating near the ship's side, the hat he had given to Leggatt. This "saving mark" confirms that the ship is sailing out of danger. With the secret stranger gone, the captain is left alone with his ship at last, enjoying "the perfect communion of a seaman with his first command." He walks to the taffrail and catches a final "evanescent glimpse" of the white floppy hat, left behind to mark the spot where the captain's "secret sharer," his "second self," had "lowered himself into the water to take his punishment: a free man, a proud swimmer striking out for a new destiny."

10

Victory

In "The Secret Sharer," Conrad explored the psychology of two young seamen—one, the narrator/captain, who succeeded in establishing his authority over his ship and himself; the other, Leggatt, whose self-possession in spite of his unlawful action posed an example for the initiate captain. In contrast, Conrad's late novel *Victory* (1915) is, among other things, the story of a man who tried to abdicate thinking as well as acting, one whose austere tastes and habits were strengthened by the bleak example of his philosopher father who had taught him to "look on—make no sound."[1]

Axel Heyst, the protagonist of *Victory*, was characterized by Conrad in his author's note as "the man of universal detachment" who "loses his mental self-possession, that fine attitude before the universally irremediable which wears the name of stoicism." In his detachment Heyst had lost the

readiness of mind and the turn of the hand that come without reflection and lead the man to excellence in life, in art, in crime, in virtue and for the matter of that, even in love. Thinking is the great enemy of perfection. The habit of profound reflection, I am compelled to say, is the most pernicious of all the habits formed by the civilized man.

Conrad's somber statement, written a few years after the book's publication, fairly reflects a view held consistently by Conrad throughout his artistic career. In fact, the novel besides being a work of instrinsic value provides a fitting reprise of many of the themes explored earlier. Here again is implied Conrad's dictum that the unconscious life is best, at least for those who are fortunate and able. Axel Heyst, however, is cursed with bad luck, he thinks too much, and his thoughts trip on unexpected impulses.

Part 1 of the novel, comprising some sixty pages, opens with a psychological pastiche of Axel Heyst furnished by the unnamed Marlow-like narrator.[2] Heyst, a mysterious Swede rumored to be a baron, has retreated from the world to the small East Indian island of Samburan. Only once during his earlier years of wandering in the "magic circle" of Southeast Asia has he been seduced from his "unattached, floating existence." In Portuguese Timor, he had appeared to Morrison, captain of the impounded *Capricorn*, as an "amazing emissary of Providence." His generous impulse in paying Morrison's fine was rewarded by an offer to share in his trading ventures, including a coal mining enterprise on Samburan, with Heyst as island manager. But Morrison died suddenly, the coal company was liquidated, and Heyst dropped out of sight.

Now the narrator learns from Captain Davidson that Heyst, living a hermit's existence on Samburan, has made a brief visit to Surabaya. But he vanishes from Schomberg's hotel, and the surly hotelkeeper will not say where. The concerned Davidson soon learns from Schomberg's wife that Heyst has left, taking with him a young Englishwoman, "a fiddle-playing girl out of an ambulant ladies' orchestra." Further, the browbeaten Mrs. Schomberg, perceiving her husband's interest in the violinist, has actually "helped the girl to bolt." A few months after the girl's rescue, the narrator meets Davidson, who recounts another visit to Samburan during which Heyst expressed regret that he had been "tempted into action."

Conrad's narrator now takes the reader back to the time of Heyst's brief stay at Schomberg's hotel. More precisely, Conrad commandeers the analysis of Heyst's disenchantment with "life as a whole." It is in this vulnerable mood that Heyst discovers the girl he will christen Lena. Heyst is drawn one night to enter Schomberg's concert hall, and during the interval he watches as the pianist strides over to a young member of the orchestra. He observes just enough to intuit that the big woman has brutally pinched the young musician. The young woman confirms the physical assault—"It wouldn't have been the first time. And suppose she did— what are you going to do about it?" And Heyst is seduced into another involvement with humanity. Conrad pointedly links Heyst's unthinking action with the impulse that years before led him to go to the aid of Morrison, but adds that this "plunge" is likely to lead to "a very different kind of partnership."

As Heyst learns more about the girl, he cannot defend himself from compassion for her friendless situation and from a mounting conscience at the growing threat posed by Schomberg's unconcealed desire for her. He is further dismayed to discover that he is attracted to her himself. He is further disconcerted when the girl puts herself in his arms and with simple directness proposes to live with him. "That disturbing night" with Lena shakes him from his detached existence, and he takes her away with him to his island.

The hotel keeper, meanwhile, is left nursing his jealous rage, his mind "perverted by the pangs of wounded vanity and of thwarted passion." The agents of Schomberg's moral corruption are an unpleasant trio who invade his hotel, and within a short time they have cowed him into permitting a gambling casino. The unsavory strangers are led by Mr. Jones, "an insolent spectre on leave from Hades" who acts as banker. His croupier is Martin Ricardo, "stealthy, desperate wild-cat turned into a man." The card-playing patrons are served by "the hairy Pedro, carrying a tray with the clumsiness of a creature caught in the woods and taught to walk on its hind legs."

Schomberg, desiring to free his hotel of their menace, directs their attention to Heyst's alleged hoard of money, and part 2 of the novel ends with his success in persuading them that the pillage of Heyst's island is both desirable and feasible.

In the third section of the book, Conrad drops the device of limited narrator, and as omniscient author opens with a description of the situation on Samburan, which for Heyst is becoming a troubled paradise. He feels that by his impulsive action in freeing the girl he has betrayed the rational counsels of his father who had urged total detachment, a contempt for hope and belief. In long conversations with Lena, Heyst recounts his efforts to play the role of unconcerned spectator. Unconscious of the ironic parallel with his relation to Lena, he tells her about Morrison who, in his eyes, was a pathetic victim of "the Great Joke," whom he had served as "an agent of Providence." He adds: "One gets attached in a way to people one has done something for. But is that friendship? I am not sure what it was. I only know that he who forms a tie is lost."

The problem for Heyst is that in rescuing Lena he has formed an attachment that he has not learned how to deal with. In her simple and direct way, Lena has responded fully to her rescuer. But Heyst has stopped short of an unreserved commitment to Lena. Still unable to declare to Lena his love, yet vulnerable to her sexual appeal, he embraces her in a sudden and unwonted access of faith in the future, and he assures her that "nothing can break in on us here." At this moment, as Heyst feels the responsive clasp of Lena's arms about his neck, Wang the Chinese servant brings news of the arrival of Schomberg's three emissaries of evil. Heyst understands that with the intruders' arrival, "the outer world" has broken in on them.

Conrad devotes the remaining pages of the third section to an extended dialogue between Martin Ricardo and his "governor," Mr. Jones, in which the author endeavors to humanize these moral monsters and at the same time rationalize their criminal behavior in ways conformable to the plot demands of the final section of the book. Although the scene contains some implausibilities, there is a fascination in the way Conrad exposes the sensibilities and the convoluted morality of these "lawless natures."

In part 4 of the novel, Conrad carries the reader to the tragic denouement through more than a hundred pages of intensifying psychological analysis interspersed with quick melodramatic bursts of action. Ricardo is shown on the prowl, drawn toward the bungalow where Lena is sequestered, his head "swimming a little with the repressed desire of violence." Armed with a knife strapped beneath his pants leg, he detects Lena behind a curtained door, and with feral instinct aroused, he charges, "head down, straight at the curtain."

With a fine piece of indirection Conrad allows the reader to learn about Ricardo's assault through the consciousness of Wang, who hears "the strange, deadened scuffling sounds" and silently departs. Back in the house, with a cinemalike strategy, Ricardo is shown "feeling his throat with tender care," breathing out admiringly: "You have fingers like steel." For Lena has thrown back his attack and sits facing him. Ricardo, his murderous impulse quelled in his new respect for Lena, abruptly confides details of the sinister quest for Heyst's "plunder." And she, electing a course of dangerous duplicity, easily convinces Ricardo that he has enlisted her against Heyst.

Heyst, for his part, is dismayed when Wang abdicates, taking with him their only weapon. And he is further shaken when he visits Jones and receives new evidence of malice. In veiled language reminiscent of Gentleman Brown's insinuations that Lord Jim shared a similar criminal past, Jones taunts Heyst: "We pursue the same ends," he said, "only perhaps I pursue them with more openness than you—with more simplicity."

Meanwhile, Ricardo is experiencing a subtle alienation from Jones. Confident that he has won Lena as a partner, and aware of his master's fierce misogyny, Ricardo has kept from him the fact of a woman's existence on the island. Ricardo has contrived to arrange a card game between Jones and Heyst, and he delivers Heyst; then he slips back to Lena's bungalow.

Heyst soon finds that the game he is playing with Jones is a far more serious one than écarté. With allegorical portentousness, Jones tells him: "Yes, I am the world itself, come to pay you a visit." And he adds: "You mustn't be shocked if I tell you plainly that we are after your money."

Heyst denies having any wealth and proposes that it was really revenge for Heyst's stealing Lena away from Schomberg that had driven the hotel keeper to mislead his guest gamblers. This is the first news that Jones has of Lena's presence on the island, and he flies into a rage. He declares a truce with Heyst and they return to Lena's bungalow. The woman-hating Jones's immediate purpose is to shoot his faithless "secretary," Ricardo. He takes aim and commands Heyst: "Stoop a little."

The reader now learns that on returning to the Heyst bungalow, Ricardo has found Lena waiting for him. The murderous suitor proposes an alliance of the two of them against Heyst and Jones, and pledges to use his knife on both. In his lover's pride he shows her the knife. Conrad's rhetoric mounts as he describes the moment when she bends forward to receive the weapon: "She had done it! The very sting of death was in her hands; the venom of the viper in her paradise, extracted, safe in her possession—and the viper's head all but lying under her heel." Having employed the knife as a powerful symbol of emasculation, Conrad makes an astonishing leap from biblical image to fantastic fetish as Ricardo bends in subjection to kiss Lena's foot.

At this moment Jones fires at his henchman, and Ricardo, grazed by Jones's bullet, runs out into the darkness. But, as the reader learns with Heyst, it is Lena who has received the fatal bullet in her breast. And it is Captain Davidson who returns in time to be able to report, presumably to Conrad's resurrected narrator, that Lena, realizing she has been shot, appeals to Heyst:

"Oh, my beloved, . . . I've saved you! Why don't you take me into your arms and carry me out of this lonely place?"

Heyst bent low over her, cursing his fastidious soul, which even at that moment kept the true cry of love from his lips in its infernal mistrust of all life. . . .

"Who else could have done this for you?" she whispered gloriously.

"No one in the world," he answered her in a murmur of unconcealed despair.

When Lena tries to raise herself, Heyst, "with a terrified and gentle movement," slips an arm under her neck, and

She felt relieved at once of an intolerable weight, and was content to surrender to him the infinite weariness of her tremendous achievement. . . . The flush of rapture flooding her whole being broke out in a smile of innocent, girlish happiness; and with that divine radiance on her lips she breathed her last, triumphant, seeking for his glance in the shades of death.

It appears that Lena's triumph, like the illusions of Jim and his double Gentleman Brown, is the only victory that Conrad can offer.

The final pages of the novel comprise a summary report supplied by Davidson to a curious official in the Archipelago. Jones had had another chance to shoot Ricardo, and this time had not missed. Later Jones's body was discovered in the waters where he had apparently tumbled from the wharf. Wang, who used Heyst's revolver to kill Pedro, had brought his Alfura woman back to his hut. And the Swedish Baron Axel Heyst had shut himself in his bungalow with Lena's body and committed a fiery suicide.

His last recorded words are reported to the official: "Ah, Davidson, woe to the man whose heart has not learned while young to hope, to love—and to put its trust in life!" But, significantly, the last word in the novel is given to Davidson himself, who remarks: "There was nothing to be done there. . . . Nothing!"

So the book ends with a characteristic Conradian seal on a characteristic Conradian theme—the futility of human activity.

11

Lingard the Rescuer

Critics have long noted a persistent motif in Conrad's late fiction—that of the rescue of a damsel in distress. This romantic theme is present in *Chance* (where the two parts of the novel are actually named "Damsel" and "Knight") as well as in *The Arrow of Gold* (1919) and in his last novel, *The Rover* (1923). In *Victory*, it was exhibited in Axel Heyst's doomed endeavor to bring Lena away to sanctuary on his island. But this chivalric aspect of Conrad's literary sensibility became evident very early in his career when he began work on "The Rescuer," a manuscript he would ultimately torture into the very late book called *The Rescue* (1920).

And Tom Lingard, the "rescuer,"[1] is a pivotal figure in any consideration of Conrad's career-long development. Captain Lingard appeared briefly in the first novel, *Almayer's Folly*, and took an increasingly important role in the second book, *An Outcast of the Islands*. Now, in a work over which Conrad struggled for more than twenty-three years, Lingard moves into the center of his fictional vision.

An earlier chapter has detailed how Conrad's conception of Charlie Marlow changed as he moved that important character from story to story. Shifts in Conrad's conception of Tom Lingard occurred also. And, allowing that the Marlow stories are justly preferred, the Lingard books are still worthy of the close attention of those who would understand the creative impulses that moved Conrad, from the 1880s, when while shipping on the *Vidar* in the Dutch East Indies he was still collecting material for his Malayan novels, until 1919, when he at last finished *The Rescue*.

My intention here, after a brief consideration of the char-

acter as he appeared in the first two novels, is to examine the
Lingard of *The Rescue,* the final form of the novel as published in 1919 at the end of Conrad's long struggle with the
book and the character. My special purpose will be to show
Lingard's growth toward an awareness of evil within himself
as well as in the world about him. Viewed in this way, *The
Rescue* may be seen as a reprise of Conrad's thematic concern
with a shift from false self-awareness to a tragic sense of
awareness beyond one's ability.

Lingard of *Almayer's Folly*

Conrad's fictional Lingard exists for scarcely twenty-five
pages in his first novel, at the beginning of a rather brief
book. In the tenth paragraph of *Almayer's Folly,* the omniscient author announces that among those "bold spirits" who
fitted out schooners in Australia and "invaded the Malay
Archipelago in search of money and adventure," Tom Lingard was recognized by the Malays as " 'the Rajah-Laut'—
the King of the Sea." Recklessly brave, impulsively generous,
loud and innocently boastful, Lingard was also enterprising
and resourceful. He was a legend for his trading successes,
his half-caste "loves," and his victories over Sulu pirates.
From the pirates he had captured a native girl, adopted her,
and sent her to be educated in "some convent in Java." He
had also discovered an entrance to the Pantai River and was
growing wealthy by taking his brig, the *Flash,* up his secret
channel for rich loads of "gutta-percha and rattans, pearl
shells and birds' nests, wax and gum-dammar." Further, he
had sworn "a mighty oath" to marry his "daughter" to a
white man "before he went home and to leave her all his
money."

This is the man who "by the boldness and enormous profits
of his ventures" becomes a hero in the eyes of the title character, Kaspar Almayer. Lingard first offers Almayer a job as
supercargo and then suddenly, in a scene of broadest comedy,
he proposes that the young man marry his ward.

The remainder of *Almayer's Folly* is an account of how
Lingard's plans for his protégés go ironically awry.[2] The man

himself returns from a disastrous expedition, aged and ill but "enthusiastic," and then goes away, taking the child of Almayer and his Malay wife. He writes once from Singapore to say that Nina is being cared for, and to announce that he is going to Europe "to raise money for the great enterprise." Almayer receives one letter more—"Then came a complete silence. Europe had swallowed up the Rajah Laut apparently, and Almayer looked vainly westward for a ray of light out of the gloom of his shattered hopes."

Such is the epitaph, in *Almayer's Folly*, of Captain Tom Lingard.

Lingard of *An Outcast of the Islands*

Early in *An Outcast of the Islands*, while supplying the psychology of Peter Willems's relationship with his wife's family, Conrad remarks ironically that in feeding and clothing the numerous and shabby Da Souzas, "he was their providence," and he adds: "It is a fine thing to be a providence, and to be told so on every day of one's life." Thus the author first announced his ironic theme of providence, a theme to be developed on several levels throughout the book, as well as in other works to follow.

For a brief time Willems plays God to the Da Souzas. But the chief God-figure in this second book is Captain Lingard. He acts as providence to Willems and also to Almayer, who is resurrected from Conrad's first novel. At the very end of *An Outcast of the Islands*, with Willems dead and other principals ruined, Almayer engages in a drinking bout with his Romanian guest, who hiccoughs, "You have a quarrel with Providence. . . ." On this same page, we learn that Lingard, who has bumbled all the way through this novel, has sailed for Europe and disappeared, as in *Almayer's Folly*. Conrad, with his ingenuity for doubling (and tripling), arranges it so that Almayer asks three pages later, "Where's your Providence? Where's the good for anybody in all this?" And he concludes, "The world's a swindle!"

This parodic image of an ineffective and fruitless providence Conrad used again and again in his many books not only as a symbol of human failure but also as an emblem of cosmic futility.

Now it is not to be expected that a character designed as a parody of providence, as Lingard clearly is, would show much deepening of insight in the course of a piece of fiction. Dickens and a few others, including Smollett, always at the risk of sentimentality, have managed some development in comic character on fairly rare occasions. That is exactly what Conrad succeeds in doing in this book with Tom Lingard, a likable but ridiculous seaman who inspires pathos as well as humor. Known for "his reckless generosity, for his unswerving honesty," Lingard has won great popularity "after his first—and successful—fight with the sea robbers, when he rescued, as rumor had it, the yacht of some big wig from home."[3]

Tom Lingard, the omniscient author states, is a master, lover, and servant of the sea, which has given him his "stupidly guileless heart." The providence motif surfaces as Conrad adds that the sea also gave Lingard "his absurd faith in himself, his universal love of creation."

Among the many who regard Lingard as their providential divinity is his agent in Sambir, Kaspar Almayer, a sullen beneficiary of Lingard's erratic generosity. The arrival of Willems as a new favorite fills Almayer with uneasiness at the thought that he may be "left outside the scheme of creation." Unknown to Almayer, Lingard fourteen years before had helped the young runaway find his first situation, with Hudig & Co., where he had risen to the position of confidential clerk. Now Willems has ruined himself by embezzling money, and Lingard has intervened because of "the whisper of his own absurd conscience." But in a few short months Willems betrays Lingard's secret channel to Lingard's rival Abdullah and pilots the Arabs up the river to Sambir. The old seaman's reaction is characteristic. He tells Willems: "I picked you up as a boy, and consider myself responsible for you in a way." And he warns him not "to quarrel with me, my boy."

Almayer, Lingard's other protégé, fulfills his part in the parody by quarreling with his providence—he blasphemes his "father" with a catalog of contemptuous accusations, and concludes with the charge that Willems's treachery has ruined Lingard—"your day is over in Sambir." The scene continues with a piece of pure burlesque comedy when a bluebottle fly distracts the two men, and the chapter ends with a hint for a burlesque theodicy as Almayer puts an implied question to his providence: "I wonder what such damned things are made for!"

Meanwhile, Lingard's troubles with the Malay leaders and the Arab invaders are complicated by the shipwreck of his beloved *Flash*, but with his benevolent instinct for "shaping stray lives he found here and there under his busy hand" he arranges to bring Willems's wife and child to Sambir and thus dooms the ineffectual paradise of Willems and Aïssa.

Conrad here pauses in his story to insert an ironic little essay on futility, followed by a long paragraph recapitulating his characterization of Lingard as a man who "had never hesitated in his life," but who now experiences "doubt and unhappiness." The old seaman has "dreamed of Arcadian happiness for that little corner of the world which he loved to think all his own," has been proud of his creation: "He loved it all." (Cf. Genesis 1:10—"And God saw that it was good.") Now, perplexed and angry, he thinks of Willems "ranging over the islands and disturbing the universe," and even contemplates destroying this latest of his works.

Part 4 of the novel, in which Lingard moves to execute justice, contains some of Conrad's best writing.[4] The scene in which he attacks Willems in a blind fury is a worthy antecedent of Camus's surrealist achievement in *The Stranger*. Following the brief violent encounter between the two men, Lingard rages at Willems, his "mistake"; and, says Conrad, the breath of his own words "fanned the spark of divine folly in his breast." He sentences Willems and departs, a defeated providence, leaving Willems to bitter exile in an Eden filled with the recriminations of its Adam and Eve. In the fifth and final section of the book, Death will enter a paradise already invaded by Evil. The last the reader sees of Lingard, in this book, he throws himself back in fatigue as his canoe bears him to the outside world.

Lingard of *The Rescue*

Perhaps the chief irony in the career of Joseph Conrad is the
fact that the book that cost him most in anguished expen-
diture of energy and exposed him to a long and savage attrition of defeat and despair is the book that has most
disappointed the critics.[5] To the Conrad admirer, *The Rescue*
may be disappointing; but I believe that there is to be found
amid its splendid wreckage evidence of a worthy artistic
achievement, as well as clues to the evolution of Conrad's
judgment and taste and style.[6] The real if flawed merit of this
novel is an intrinsic thing. It is also important for the way
the Lingard of this book fits into Conrad's gallery of those
who become tragically aware beyond their moral ability.

Misconceptions concerning this key figure date far back in
Conrad scholarship. John Dozier Gordan, for example, in his
pioneer study of 1940, included *The Rescue* among Conrad's
"unshirking studies of human disintegration," and declared
that Conrad "unfalteringly" traced the "subtle deterioration
of Lingard and Mrs. Travers." But readers who persevere to
the end of *The Rescue* will have Conrad's parting view of
Edith Travers, who "stood aft very rigid," grasping the rail
of her husband's yacht as it sailed due south, and they will
read Lingard's bleak command: "Steer north." If they read
with intelligent sympathy, they will feel that Gordan erred in
grouping this man and woman with Almayer, Willems, and
the "sinister Belgian agents" in "Heart of Darkness" and "An
Outpost of Progress."[7]

Vernon Young, writing in 1953 on "Lingard's Folly: The
Lost Subject," declared that Conrad's two Malayan novels
and *The Rescue* "comprise what might have been a purposeful
trilogy, a tragedy in three acts, centered in the character of
Tom Lingard." Young noted that Albert Guerard, in 1947,
had accepted "the trilogy as an essay in moral continuity."
Then, unaccountably, Young synopsized the three novels in
reverse order, to establish a strict chronological order for the
career of Lingard.[8] Guerard was certainly correct in sensing
a moral and psychological continuity in the three novels, but
this cannot be understood in terms of a factitious chronology

of Lingard's career.[9] I believe that the books should be read in the order that they were written, accepting the simple paradox that in his passage from the two early Malay novels to the final book of the "trilogy," Lingard *matures* as he *grows younger.*

Thomas Moser, who had the advantage of examining the early manuscript, "The Rescuer," devoted his analysis to proving that the novel represents a lapse in creative power on the part of the later Conrad. Perhaps this is so. But to summarize the manuscript version as the story of "an egoistic white man who meddles in native politics for the sake of a young Celebes prince and his sister" and then, taking a false lead from Conrad's correspondence, to charge that in his final version the author introduced the European "yacht people to please the public" is to come close to suggesting that Conrad's art is meretricious.[10]

Moser, who believed that sex was the "uncongenial subject" for Conrad, thought that the author abandoned "The Rescuer" because he could not write the love story of Lingard and Mrs. Travers.[11] However that may be, it is clear that Conrad meant to leave no doubt there was a powerful physical attraction between this man and woman.

The first time Lingard notices Edith Travers he is stirred to unconscious depths, convinced

that of all the women he knew, she alone seemed to be made for action. Every one of her movements had firmness, ease, the meaning of a vital fact, the moral beauty of a fearless expression. Her supple figure was not dishonoured by any faltering of outlines under the plain dress of dark blue stuff moulding her form with bold simplicity.

When he talks with her about their serious predicament, his mental processes are short-circuited as his eyes wander over the lines of her body. He knows that "he must do something. . . . What should he do? Instead of answering that question he traced the ungleaming coils of her twisted hair and became fascinated by a stray lock at her neck." He is seduced by her voice, which he thinks "very commanding and very sweet." And he "took her spiritually for granted," but it was "materially"—that is, physically—that Edith Travers was a wonder:

What pleased him most was her not looking at him; for it enabled him to contemplate with perfect freedom the curve of her cheek, her small ear half hidden by the clear mesh of fine hair, the fascination of her uncovered neck. And her whole person was an impossible, an amazing and solid marvel which somehow was not so much convincing to the eye as to something within him that was apparently independent of his senses.

Considering that the events of this story supposedly took place about 1860 and that the author himself lived in a time when bikinis were unheard of, this seems to be about as far as opportunity would permit Lingard to go in his physical appraisal of Mrs. Travers.

In his comparison of "The Rescuer" with the published novel, Moser cited "certain crucial cuts from the original manuscript" to show how Conrad managed "the simplification and emasculation of Lingard."[12] And more recently psychoanalytic techniques have been utilized to explain Conrad's allegedly uncomfortable demeanor when handling the subject of sex.[13] What is important here is for us to understand that, regardless of personal distaste or any other inhibiting factor, the artist in Conrad was working in this book to show the powerful sexual element in Lingard's relationship with Mrs. Travers.

Consider for instance how he depicts Lingard when it appears that Edith Travers is going along with his plan to move the yacht passengers to the safety of his brig. Conrad's description of the man as he exultantly prepares the defense of the ship is loaded with erotic imagery:

He took a musket down, loaded it, then took another and another. He hammered at the waddings with fierce joyousness. The ramrods rang and jumped. It seemed to him he was doing his share of some work in which that woman was playing her part faithfully. "She has done it," he repeated mentally. "She will sit in the cuddy. She will sleep in my berth."

Later, as events move toward disaster, Lingard seeks her out because "he actually needed her bodily presence." On a "night full of roused passions and deadly purposes," Edith Travers comes to Lingard in the enemy compound, and Conrad makes plain *her* physical response. In the darkness, she hears his voice directing her: "It vibrated through all her fibres, rousing like the call of a trumpet, went far beyond her, filled all the space. Mrs. Travers stood still for a moment, then casting far away from her the burning torch ran forward blindly with her hands extended toward the great sound of Lingard's voice."

Stopped by the stockade, she endures a moment of terror— "Was she to be transfixed by a broad blade, to the high, immovable wall of wood against which she was flattening herself desperately . . . ?" The imagery of sex continues:

Lingard's voice somewhere from the sky above her head was directing her, distinct, very close, full of concern.

"You must stoop low. Lower yet."

The stagnant blood of her body began to pulsate languidly.

Lingard speaks again, and

she put her head and shoulders through the opening, was at once seized under the arms by an eager grip and felt herself pulled through with an irresistible force and with such haste that her scarf was dragged off her head, its fringes having caught in the rough timber. . . . He didn't release his hold of her; his helpful and irresistible grip had changed into a close clasp, a crushing embrace, the violent taking possession by an embodied force that had broken loose and was not to be controlled any longer. As his great voice had done a moment before, his great strength, too, seemed able to fill all space in its enveloping and undeniable authority. Every time she tried instinctively to stiffen herself against its might, it reacted, affirming its fierce will, its uplifting power.

Conrad reminds the reader that reckless passion has driven this woman to join Lingard. Now, to her, the man is "like a blind force. She closed her eyes altogether. Her head fell back a little. Not instinctively but with wilful resignation and as it were from a sense of justice she abandoned herself to his arms." Thus does Conrad delineate the complexly motivated response of this highly civilized woman.

And the effect of her subtle act of surrender upon Lingard is credible. He lets her go "so suddenly and completely that she would have fallen down in a heap if she had not managed to catch hold of his forearm."

Critics who read signs of Conrad's sexual reserve in his admittedly awkward love scenes doubtless deem it unsatisfactory that Lingard and Mrs. Travers did not consummate their passion—even that Conrad did not somehow break through Victorian convention to make plain that Edith Travers's levator leaped, that Lingard's phallic reflexes were in operating order.[14]

They should at least credit him with doing what he could to show the contrasting masculine and feminine afterresponses to their sexual encounter. Edith is left with a sense of relief and release—"a period of peace without thought," and she searches for a lost sandal ("symbolic as a dropped veil"). "She had been carried off the earth, without shame, without regret." The man and woman confront each other, "he rigid in an effort of self-command but feeling as if the surges of the heaviest sea that he could remember in his life were running through his heart; and the woman as if emptied of all feeling by her experience, without thought yet, but beginning to regain her sense of the situation."

I conclude my discussion of this topic with a little fret that a critic like Moser would charge on the one hand that Conrad "emasculates" Lingard, and a critic like Frederick Karl on the other hand would insinuate that he is somehow less heroic, less masculine because passion affects his moral decisions.[15]

Still other misconceptions show up in Moser's four-point analysis of the "simplification and emasculation" of Lingard's character as presented in "The Rescuer" manuscript.[16] According to Moser, Conrad's alterations of "The Rescuer" obscured "the most important and interesting facts of Lingard's psychology: the subtle difference between himself and other seamen, his egoistic longings for power, his lack of self-knowledge, his moral isolation."[17]

The evidence Moser cited to show that certain "unseamanlike" traits had been erased indicates simply that Conrad excised passages that tended to stress questionable, even lawless, aspects of his adventurer-hero. These refinements, I believe, could be construed as strengthening the author's chances of creating a sympathetic portrait without reducing the hero to absolute conventionality. Second, Moser argued that *The Rescue* omits "the most important of Lingard's motives—his egoism."[18] I am convinced that Lingard, as much as any Conradian figure, bears the last infirmity of an egocentric hero. Doggedly he clings throughout the novel to his honor: "I have my name to take care of. Everything rests on that."

As to Lingard's "lack of self-knowledge," I believe that the movement of this novel is steadily away from the portrait of stupid and impulsive innocence in *Almayer's Folly* or the meddling providence of *An Outcast of the Islands*.[19] Gone is the comic view of providence parodied, characteristic of Conrad's earlier, external view of Lingard. As the author moves *inside* Tom Lingard the tone modulates from comic to potentially tragic. When the "world of his creation" goes to pieces, it is the world of a mortal man. Lingard is no longer a burlesque deity—he is Conrad's attempt to set forth a human being, albeit as d'Alcacer reads him, "a rough man naively engaged in a contest with heaven's injustice."

Lingard, in *The Rescue*, begins "unaware"—the word is Conrad's; he also calls him "unconscious of everything and everybody." He is "the man ready for the obvious, no matter how startling, how terrible or menacing, yet defenceless as a child before the shadowy impulses of his own heart."

Confronted by the intractability of the men on the yacht and, ultimately, even in his relationship with Mrs. Travers feeling the subtle threat of incompatibility, he sulkily insists: "I am what I am." Then, when young Carter unwittingly breaks the compact by firing on the warpraus of the natives, Lingard tells Edith Travers, "I am nothing now." To Lingard,

Carter's blunder "was a blow struck straight at his heart"—
but

he was not angry with Carter. . . . In this fatality Carter was a mere
incident. The real cause of the disaster was somewhere else. . . .
And at the same time Lingard could not defend himself from a
feeling that it was in himself, too, somewhere in the unexplored
depths of his nature, something fatal and unavoidable.

Conrad, who enough times is brilliantly indirect, is here
persistently obvious. Lingard mutters, "No. I am not a lucky
man." And the author continues, somewhat ponderously:

He was not the man to give himself up to the examination of his
own sensations. . . . Conflict of some sort was the very essence of
his life. But this was something he had never known before. This
was a conflict within himself. He had to face unsuspected powers,
foes that he could not go out to meet at the gate. They were within,
as though he had been betrayed by somebody, by some secret
enemy. He was ready to look round for that subtle traitor. A sort
of blankness fell on his mind and he suddenly thought: "Why! It's
myself."

Possibly, as Moser said, Conrad mistakenly eliminated certain passages of "The Rescuer" manuscript, yet enough remains in *The Rescue* to show Lingard moving from ignorance
to self-knowledge and awareness.

Moser stated his fourth charge: "A final, important insight
into Lingard that the later Conrad finds of no use is the
increasing isolation that results from his egoistic involvement
in an unlawful adventure."[20] The unlawful aspects of Lingard's adventure and of his personality have indeed been
refined by Conrad's revisions. But the *isolation* survives and
deepens. From the beginning of the story, Lingard feels re-
pelled by the bigoted Shaw, the only European in his crew.
Except for Mrs. Travers and Carter, he is never drawn to the
Europeans on the yacht. Lingard experiences a progressive
alienation from Hassim and Immada and all their native allies.
The final break with Mrs. Travers, in spite of their mutual

appeal for each other, is inevitable. At the end of the book he walks on the beach "by himself, feeling a stranger to all men and abandoned by the All-Knowing God." Even though he has gained a competent and loyal mate in young Carter, it is unlikely that the young man will ever invade the isolation of the lonely man who commands him.

Incidentally, and mystifyingly, arguing that Carter "suffers even more seriously from Lingard's emasculation," Moser remarks: "As originally conceived in 'The Rescuer,' he belongs in the company of Singleton and MacWhirr. He is the calmest person aboard Travers's yacht, but also the one most aware of its dangerous position. He approaches all problems practically and unemotionally. Although he is as young as Jukes and Jim, he differs from them in his readiness to meet unexpected disasters."[21]

Well—perhaps. But what Moser failed anywhere to note is that Carter does not have the good fortune of unconscious Singleton or MacWhirr. Carter, out of a confusion of loyalty, ignorance, and mistrust, is the very person who *creates* the disaster in *The Rescue* by his unprovoked attack on the natives.

But it is easy to read past Conrad's subtle qualifiers when he is being his most ironic self. Following the disaster, Carter finds Lingard in the cabin of the brig, and " 'I never expected to see any of you alive,' Carter began in his easy tone, but with much less carelessness in his bearing as though his days of responsibility amongst the Shoals of the Shore of Refuge had matured his view of the external world and of his own place therein."

As though . . . ? Is Conrad hinting that Carter never realizes his own moral blunder?

What then is the thematic achievement of *The Rescue?* There are many themes, among them the ironic consequence of Lingard's decision to "rescue" the yacht passengers. At the end of the book, even the uncomprehending Carter, in his half-knowledge, sympathizes with "that man who had certainly rescued the white people but seemed to have lost his own soul in the attempt." Another theme relates precisely to that half-knowledge that hounds every important character in this and other Conrad novels. But more important in *The Rescue* than in any other work of Conrad is a theme itself bound up in the frustrations of knowledge and action: this is the theme of the severe limitations of human trust and distrust, tangled as they are with good intentions, a strong sense of obligation, partial knowledge, and impulsive actions—all, and at all times, imperiled by irremediable evil.

Lack of trust is chronic in this book. From the start Lingard withheld plans from his first mate Shaw, the only other European aboard his brig. It is Shaw who leads Carter, the yacht's mate, to mistrust Lingard's intentions. Eventually Mrs. Travers's trust in Lingard, inspired by his faith in her, leads Carter to "surrender to that man." But Lingard, while in turn trusting Carter, is impelled to withhold essential facts from Carter. Later when disaster strikes, Lingard acknowledges to Mrs. Travers that Carter had not been taken into full confidence.

Daman, Lingard's fierce and unpredictable Illanun ally, "does not know how to trust anyone." Belarab, the native chieftain, who suffers from a "mistrust of the universe," is first to understand that his white friend is being betrayed by Tengga and his followers. Pata Hassim and Immada, the noble exiles for whom Lingard has worked long and futilely, at last come to doubt Lingard. And Lingard, the man who had assured his native friends, "I will not fail you," who has said to the whites, "I will see you through all safe if you will only trust me," comes to understand that he does not know his own mind, and that he is capable of forgetting Hassim and Immada not once, but twice. Seduced by his love for Edith Travers, he is snarled in distrust of himself and of others.

Conrad roots the tragedy of this man in the circumstances of his first meetings with the natives and with the whites. His early encounter with Hassim and Immada has created in him a complex sense of responsibility, which he certified with explicit promises. And, for two years, plans are developed on their behalf. Then with the sudden appearance of the European yacht in the shallows off the Shore of Refuge he is confronted with *their* trust, with the "unconscious demand of these people's presence."

This leads to the other side of the coin of trust and distrust, as minted by Conrad. If distrust compounds the circumstances of disaster, *trust* also, in the view of Conrad, can be a treacherous thing. From the beginning, as indicated earlier, Lingard and Edith Travers trust each other. Yet Conrad shows that Lingard, in sharing his story with Mrs. Travers is investing his trust for a return of disaster. Lingard thinks: "She stood by his side!" Conrad pronounces this to be a "fatal illusion." And Lingard's illusory faith in Edith Travers's fidelity leads first to the bitter illumination in the woman's consciousness. At the very moment she withholds from Lingard the crucial fact that she has Hassim's ring, she thinks: "He believes in me."

A further irony resides in the fact that her distrust of Jorgenson contributes to her unwitting suppression of the ring's silent message that Hassim and Immada have been captured. With Lingard's head on her knee, she suppresses her impulse to tell him of the ring—"Why should she torment him with all those questions of freedom and captivity, of violence and intrigue, of life and death?"—and thus betrays Lingard and herself as well. The culmination of this tragic pattern of misplaced trust mingled with forestalling distrust comes in the consciousness of Lingard when he learns from the dying Jaffir of Mrs. Travers's betrayal. Even so, he admits to the dying man that even "if she had given the ring to me it would have been to one that was dumb, deaf, and robbed of all courage."

Variations on the theme of the paralyzing force of distrust and the fatal consequence of faith misplaced and trust betrayed are to be found in still other characters in *The Rescue*. There are implications in Jorgenson's "mistrust and contempt for the life of men" and in the ultimate untrustworthiness of this man who, ironically doubling Lingard, never broke his word "to white or native." Also, the ignorant and conceited Travers, who once observed that his wife "inspired mistrust" in the society of the other side of the world, and the intelligent but disaffected d'Alcacer, who counseled Mrs. Travers to

withhold the ring, both participate in the pattern of irre-
sponsibility and faithlessness.[22]

Importantly, Edith Travers in her own way suffers the same
tragic disillusion that overtakes Lingard. Conditioned by her
European background to a passive attitude toward "the necessities of existence," she perceives that "the world is too
prudent to be sincere." Hating conventions that trammel "the
frankness of her own impulses," she envies Immada, the native princess, because "nothing stood between that girl and
the truth of her sensations." Mrs. Travers is "alert to perceive
what is intrinsically great and profound within the forms of
human folly," yet sees herself helplessly involved in Lingard's
folly, "as one is involved in a natural cataclysm."

In her short time with Lingard she has been "torn away
from all her certitudes." At the end, she acknowledges that
Lingard, "that man of infinite illusions," had "all the right"
on his side, and assimilating the bitter truth of her unfaithfulness, she acknowledges to d'Alcacer that Lingard is "done
with" her. She shows the fateful ring to d'Alcacer; then, sym-
bolically, she throws the "dead talisman" overboard and
bursts into tears.

Eloise Knapp Hay, in her book on Conrad's political novels, quoted at length from a letter Conrad sent to the publisher
of *Blackwood's Magazine*, in which he set forth his plan for
The Rescue. Conrad wrote in part:

The human interest of the tale is in the contact of Lingard the
simple, masterful, imaginative adventurer with a type of civilized
woman—a complex type. He is a man tenacious of purpose, enthusiastic in undertaking, faithful in friendship. He jeopardizes the
success of his plans first to assure her safety and then absolutely
sacrifices them to what he believes the necessary condition of her
happiness. He is t[h]roughout mistrusted by the whites whom he
wishes to save; he is unwillingly forced into a contest with his Malay
friends. Then when the rescue, for which he had sacrificed all the
interests of his life, is accomplished, he has to face his reward—an
inevitable separation. This episode of his life lifts him out of himself;
I want to convey in the action of the story the stress and exaltation
of the man under the influence of a sentiment which he hardly
understands and yet which is real enough as he goes on reckless of

consequences. It is only at the very last that he is perfectly enlightened when the work of rescue and destruction is ended and nothing is left to him but to try and pick up as best he may the broken thread of his life.[23]

With Ms. Hay, I agree that this is an admirable précis of the novel "as it was begun and as it was finished over twenty years later."[24] The point is that one has here Conrad's statement of intention to present a human being who strives to fulfill promises made to himself and to others; and at the last, when "the work of rescue and destruction" is finished and nothing is left to him but to try to pick up "the broken thread of his life," he is, as Conrad put it, "perfectly enlightened"—which is to say, made tragically aware beyond one's powers. It is precisely this tragic vision that Conrad wished to communicate to his readers.

12

Ordeal by Decision:
"A Choice of Nightmares"

I have tried in this book, while keeping faithful to the texts, to deal with each story from the particular moral and psychological viewpoint of the characters involved. I have tried to show an essential connection between the level of awareness experienced by Conrad's people and their respective views of right and wrong, of truth and reality, of human freedom and responsibility. I hope that I have succeeded in clarifying the nature of Conrad's vision of the world and man's place in it.

I speak here of Conrad's artistic vision, of the vision conveyed in his fiction, and not of any "official" view he may have affected in his prefaces and other public statements. This official view, fostered by early critics, is decidedly at variance with the drift of implications in the works of his early and middle periods, and even of certain prefatory remarks written in the early period. Much nearer to the authentic fictional vision is the bleak, sometimes violent pessimism of his intimate correspondence, particularly in the decade before and the decade after 1900. Coincident with the later decline of Conrad's creative powers may be detected a wavering of this grim view, even an attempt by Conrad to recover the early official faith in simple values. *The Rover*, for example, Conrad's last completed novel, is a respectable reprise of simple heroism in the romantic tradition.

It is well, perhaps, to cite some typical expressions of Conrad's "official" view and also of his franker, if more extreme, personal statements to friends. In addition, passages will be drawn from the earliest prefaces. In my sketch of Marlow, I referred to the author's note written for *Chance* in 1920, in which Conrad, speaking self-consciously and publicly, boasts that he has never been charged with sinning against "the basic feelings and elementary convictions which make life possible to the mass of mankind," and he is gratified that no one has doubted his sound belief in "the solidarity of all mankind in simple ideas and in sincere emotions." That same year, in his author's note to *The Secret Agent* Conrad inserted a disclaimer that he was other than a normally wholesome novelist, with "no perverse intention, no secret scorn for the natural sensibilities of mankind at the bottom of my impulses." This was in 1920. It was in 1912 that Conrad published, in "A Familiar Preface" to *A Personal Record,* the words that became the golden text for this official view:

"Those who read me know my conviction that the world, the temporal world, rests on a few very simple ideas; so simple that they must be as old as the hills. It rests notably, among others, on the idea of Fidelity."

The Shadow-Line, a tale of first command that Conrad called "not a story really but exact autobiography," was a moving restatement in 1917 of his ideal of courage and of fidelity to a traditional code of conduct. This unusually direct expression of faith in the simple virtues combined with Conrad's frequent public affirmations to foster the official view.

In contrast with the affirmative tone of these pronouncements, taken to heart by Conrad's readers and early critics, are some less frequently quoted remarks to be found in earlier prefaces, such as the author's note to *Almayer's Folly* and the preface to *The Nigger of the "Narcissus."* The first of these, written in 1895, Conrad allowed to stand in all later editions of *Almayer's Folly.* In it he speaks of the solidarity of mankind on all sides of the globe—"there is a bond between us and that humanity so far away." And he ends with a statement full of grim paradox: "Their hearts—like ours—must endure the load of the gifts from Heaven: the curse of facts and the blessings of illusions, the bitterness of our wisdom and the deceptive consolation of our folly."

It is, of course, in his private correspondence that Conrad

is seduced into some of his frankest expression, particularly in letters to R. B. Cunninghame Graham. One of his closest friends at that time, Cunninghame Graham was a well-known radical politician, a man of markedly differing temperament and outlook whose views presumably evoked Conrad's extreme words. To him Conrad wrote (December 20, 1897):

You are a most hopeless idealist,—your aspirations are irrealisable. You want from men faith, honour, fidelity to truth in themselves and others. You want them to have all this, to show it every day, to make out of these words their rule of life. . . . What makes you dangerous is your unwarrantable belief that your desire may be realized. This is the only point of difference between us. I do not believe.[1]

On January 14, 1898, the day after he finished reading a life of Saint Teresa, by Cunninghame Graham's wife, which also was the day before Conrad's first son, Borys, was born, the novelist wrote his friend:

The mysteries of the universe made of drops of fire and clods of mud do not concern us in the least. The fate of humanity condemned ultimately to perish from cold is not worth troubling about. If you take it to heart it becomes an unendurable tragedy. If you believe in improvement you must weep, for the attained perfection must end in cold, darkness and silence. . . .

Half the words we use have no meaning whatever and of the other half each man understands each word after the fashion of his own folly and conceit. Faith is a myth and beliefs shift like mists on the shore: . . . As our peasants say: "Pray, brother, forgive me for the love of God." And we don't know what forgiveness is, nor what is love, nor where God is.[2]

Less than a week after composing this bleak letter to Cunninghame Graham, in which are questioned "hateful" reason, the meaning of forgiveness and love, and the whereabouts of God, Conrad was giving expression to a conventional formula appropriate to his positive, public philosophy: he wrote Mme. Aniela Zagórska (January 21, 1898) commending to her his newborn son "in the name of God."[3]

Conrad soon returned to his private cynicism, writing, in February 1898, to Cunninghame Graham:

You with your ideals of sincerity, courage and truth are strangely out of place in this epoch of material preoccupations. What does it bring? What's the profit? What do we get by it? These questions are at the root of every moral, intellectual or political movement. Into the noblest cause men manage to put something of their baseness; and sometimes when I think of You here, quietly, You seem to me tragic with your courage, with your beliefs and your hopes. Every cause is tainted: and you reject this one, espouse that other one as if one were evil and the other good while the same evil you hate is in both, but disguised in different words. . . . Alas! what you want to reform are not institutions,—it is human nature.

He added: "We are born initiated, and succeeding generations clutch the inheritance of fear and brutality without a thought, without a doubt, without compunction—in the name of God."[4]

On May 1, 1898, he pronounces humans to be "fourbes, lâches, menteurs, voleurs, cruels," and on June 11, 1898, he comments: "L'ignoble boule roulera toujours portant des êtres infimes et méchants dans un univers qui ne se comprends pas lui-même."[5]

Yet between these letters, on June 3, he attempts, not too successfully, to assume his affirmative pose for the sake of a young friend's bride, Helen Watson Sanderson:

You mustn't let other things grind you at all. In these matters the great thing is to be faithfully yourself. . . . And if—at times— you feel defeated, believe me it will be a delusion, because no circumstances of man's contriving can be stronger than a personality upheld by faith and conscience. There! I wish I could say something really helpful—something practical to you—and here I am unable to present anything but a belief.[6]

Even to Helen Sanderson, within a few months (August 31, 1898), he allows his mask to slip: "My head feels as if full of sawdust. Of course many people's heads are full of sawdust—the tragic part of the business is in my being aware of it. The man who finds out that apparently innocent truth about himself is henceforth of no use to mankind. Which proves the saving power of illusions."[7]

To Mme. Zagórska, on December 18, 1898, he apologized for his "foolish and not very praiseworthy pessimism."[8] But within the week, on December 23, 1898, he wrote a letter to H. G. Wells that was full of quirky whimsicality in which he attached conventional Christmas greetings at "the time of their voicing prescribed by the superstitions of men."[9] As late as 1904, according to Jean-Aubry's dating, Conrad was warning the optimistic Wells: "Generally the fault I find with you is that you do not take sufficient account of human imbecility which is cunning and perfidious."[10]

Why then did Conrad cling to his public faith, his asserted belief in the simple virtues of mankind and in human solidarity? Partly, I think, because he realized, as he wrote John Galsworthy in 1908, that pessimism goes too far if it goes beyond pronouncement on "the vanity of things" to proclaim "the utter futility of existence." He told Galsworthy: "This is the danger of the moralist who has not a faith, however crude, distorted or extravagant, to present to his audience."[11] Conrad was warning his fellow writer of the peril of submerging one's art in absolute nihilism. What he was counseling was the need of an affirmative moral vision to sustain artistic creativity. This was Conrad's instinctive tendency in his own career. What I think he never understood was that his continual protestation of a faith was, in his best work, subverted by his artist's tragic vision.

By all accounts, Conrad's most successful and extended formal statement of his aesthetic intentions is the celebrated preface to The Nigger of the "Narcissus," which he composed in 1897. When read against the background of his privately acknowledged pessimism, this document provides startling hints of a view unsuspected by its many admirers.

Concerning the artist's appeal, Conrad wrote:

The changing wisdom of successive generations discards ideas, questions facts, demolishes theories. But the artist appeals to that part of our being which is not dependent on wisdom; to that in us which is a gift and not an acquisition—and, therefore, more permanently enduring. He speaks to our capacity for delight and wonder, to the sense of mystery surrounding our lives; to our sense of pity, and beauty, and pain; to the latent feeling of fellowship with all creation—and to the subtle but invincible conviction of solidarity that knits together the loneliness of innumerable hearts, to the solidarity in dreams, in joy, in sorrow, in aspirations, in illusions, in hope, in fear, which binds men to each other, which binds together all humanity—the dead to the living and the living to the unborn.

This "subtle but invincible conviction of solidarity," it must be clear by now, is not limited to noble companionship of the mighty heroes of life, nor yet to the easy camaraderie between us and what Marlow, in *Lord Jim,* called "that good, stupid kind we like to feel marching right and left of us in life, of the kind that is not disturbed by the vagaries of intelligence and the perversions of—of nerves, let us say."

It includes also the "unforeseen partnerships" of life—between Marlow and Jim, between Jim and Gentleman Brown, between Marlow and his helmsman, between Marlow and Kurtz, between Razumov and Haldin, between the captain/narrator and his "secret sharer," between Heyst and Lena, between Lingard and Mrs. Travers. In the terms of Karl Jaspers, "This solidarity extends even to an enemy when selfhood comes into genuine opposition with selfhood."[12] Solidarity for Conrad is not universal brotherhood. Writing to Cunninghame Graham (February 8, 1899), he asks: "Franchement what would you think of an attempt to promote fraternity amongst people living in the same street, I don't even mention two neighbouring streets? Two ends of the same street."[13]

Fictional art, Conrad wrote in the preface, rests on "the appeal of one temperament to all the other innumerable temperaments whose subtle and resistless power endows passing events with their true meaning, and creates the moral, the emotional atmosphere of the place and time."

The creative task, then, is "by the power of the written word to make you hear, to make you feel—it is, before all, to make you *see*. That—and no more, and it is everything.

If I succeed, you shall find there according to your deserts: encouragement, consolation, fear, charm—all you demand— and, perhaps, also, that glimpse of truth for which you have forgotten to ask."

Often, in Conrad's works, the unsought truth can be a tragic illumination.

In his approach to characters like Almayer, Willems, and Nostromo, and the early Lingard (of the first two Malay books), Conrad moved with a sureness sustained by ironic purpose to expose the kind of person who is ensnared in his own false image of himself and of the world. All these people are excruciatingly aware, but they are aware falsely. They are trapped in their own subjectivity. Their only duty is to themselves. All feel "betrayed" by somebody else or something outside themselves. Evil is in their world, they recognize, and as in the case of Nostromo they may refer this evil to themselves, but never in truthful terms. These characters, except for rare and fitful moments of transitory awareness, are pathetic rather than tragic. As a rule, they live unprincipled lives and die meaningless deaths.

The unconscious, the fortunate ones, those who embody the virtues esteemed in Conrad's public philosophy, include Singleton, MacWhirr, and Stein.[14] Singleton is the archetype of this admired breed of human being. He is able, lucky, faithful, unthinking, and "profound."[15] MacWhirr is equally unaware. Comic and absurd, he nevertheless operates effectively in his limited world. Endowed with just enough imagination to get through each day, he acts with unthinking courage and metes out a coarse kind of justice. He is faithful and fair, but he is disdained by destiny. Stein too is able and unconscious—and lucky, by unimpeachable testimony. He has lived his own life effectively. Yet his romantic remedy for Jim proves finally to be inadequate, and the cloudy dreamworld in which the old man lives possibly obscures from Stein his own grim role in Lord Jim's disaster.

Stein's ambiguous position helps us, in terms of moral geography, to locate Brierly and the French naval officer along the boundary between the able and unconscious and the falsely aware. Apparently Brierly was able to suppress some secret moral disaster that threatened his self-image of luck and competence.[16] Confronted by Jim's case, Brierly suffered a shattering assault upon his self-image and found that he could not bear the revelation of his moral disability. The French lieutenant, at least so far as Marlow knew to report, seems to have succeeded in repressing his moment of grim truth, and thus survived, sustained by his illusion of integrity.

We have then a range from the unconsciousness of a Singleton to the beclouded consciousness of a lucky Stein or an efficient French naval officer, supported by the drug of honor, a combination stimulant-depressant touched with a tincture of illusion. These people understand that evil is in the world, even in other people around them. They realize that this evil, in the form of hostile purposes, and preeminently in the form of death, threatens them. But they never relate to this evil in tragic awareness. They have not been made to confront moral disability in themselves.

The harsh realities of life so far as Conrad is concerned are borne by those few who are tragically aware. They include Mrs. Gould, Lingard of *The Rescue*, Edith Travers perhaps, and the Marlow of *Lord Jim* and "Heart of Darkness."[17] These men and women are people of principle. They begin with the best of humane intentions. They are open-eyed to the evil in the world and in the people with whom they must deal. At last each comes to recognize that an irremediable aspect of this evil invades oneself.

Every action means something (as Lingard said). This may not always be a preconceived notion or intellectual principle, certainly not always an expressed motive. But intentions, even when understood, and methods, even when correct, do not guarantee desirable results. And results, foreseen or unforeseen, turn out to betray calculations and commitments that in retrospect may appear unworthy. Bitterest of all for a character like Lingard, nothing fails like failure.

But, as Mrs. Gould knew, success can be morally too costly. Ignorance connives with chance and circumstances, with other purposes and powers, with the clash of good wills, with malevolence, and with raw evil to produce calamitous effects. Mrs. Gould, at the end of a long trail marked by brutality, treachery, violence, deceit, and cunning, realizes that her husband's moral idealism and her own desires have been frustrated in part by their own moral deficiencies. She is tragically aware beyond her moral ability. This tragic illumination is sealed by her suppression of facts from her husband and by her heroic lie to the prying Dr. Monygham.

Lingard does not lie intentionally, as do Mrs. Gould and Marlow. (Mrs. Travers comes nearer to Mrs. Gould's experience in this regard.) But he breaks an oath cavalierly taken; and, caught in a web of deceit, he cannot extricate himself from the tragic realization that by his actions he has reneged on promises faithfully made to his friends, with fatal consequences. He began by engaging his life in what he recognizes as a moral universe. He soon understands that force, his only weapon, has developed the aspect of treachery. He learns finally that trust leads to betrayal, that distrust leads to confusion and disaster.

Marlow comes, in Lord Jim, to acknowledge his moral kinship with Jim; and in this kinship he recognizes a capacity within himself for disabling moral actions and intentions. In "Heart of Darkness," Marlow journeys within himself, and there he finds the terms of his moral life. Truthtelling for Marlow, like promisekeeping for Lingard, is the seal of fidelity. Marlow's sensibility obliges him to state, "There is a taint of death, a flavour of mortality in lies." But at the Central Station he goes close to a lie in behalf of Kurtz; when the company official in Brussels demands Kurtz's document, Marlow tears off the damning "postscriptum" and suppresses it; and, finally, his "choice of nightmares" is certified when he helps Kurtz's Intended to preserve her saving illusions by telling her a lie.[18] Even the Marlow of Chance pays a solemn tribute to solidarity by declaring that it is better to be immoral than to be cruel.

Significantly, Marlow witnesses several "triumphs"—including those of Lord Jim, of Gentleman Brown, and of Kurtz. It would appear that Lord Jim's triumph was as illusory as that of Gentleman Brown—indeed, as illusory as the "victory" of Lena, which was recorded by a Marlow-like narrator.

In the opinion of Marlow—and I believe of Conrad also— only the "moral victory" of Kurtz was valid.

Conrad's journey away from ethical affirmation ends in a dark illumination. The precise illumination is not always clear. Its content is certainly not the same for everyone. But for everyone who *sees,* it is evil. Colonial exploitation, for example, "is not a pretty thing when you look into it much." Conrad's old-fashioned verdict is simply that human motivation inevitably taints desired good—one cannot even know one's own motivations. Virtue is uncertain, and—though Conrad would eschew the theological term—sin is sure. One's only certain freedom is the freedom to sin. One's only true knowledge is of evil. Conversely, when one truly knows, when one *sees,* one sees evil.[19] Ours is an ordeal by choosing. Resolutely one selects the good that one would save, and then resolutely one chooses its concomitant nightmare. Or, as Lingard put it to his faithful serang, Wasub—"Weapons or words? Which folly?"

The reader has come a long way from Stein's "follow the dream." The admonition of Conrad at his deepest and darkest is "Choose your own nightmare." This is the ethical consequence of tragic awareness beyond ability. Conrad early analyzed and dismissed those who are falsely aware of reality. He reluctantly came to give up those who are able only because they are lucky and unconscious, or are fortunate but befogged by romantic or other illusion. Finally he reserved his ultimate respect only for those who receive the tragic vision of evil within and without, and bravely endure the ordeal by decision, the choice of nightmares.

Perhaps not everyone is willing to accept the grim picture of reality conveyed in Conrad's artistic vision. But there is no reason to reject his notion of tragic illumination, the revelation to an individual of his or her flawed nature related ethically and ontologically to a flawed universe, and with this, an implied theory of tragedy as human awareness beyond moral ability.

Often enough Conrad is successful in his effort to make his readers see, and "the presented vision of regret or pity, of terror or mirth" does awaken in their hearts "that feeling of unavoidable solidarity; of the solidarity of mysterious origin, in toil, in joy, in hope, in uncertain fate, which binds men to each other and all mankind to the visible world."

And the tragic illumination, in a few cases, provides one with "that glimpse of truth" for which one forgot to ask.

Notes

Chapter 1: Biography

1. Although he adopted "Joseph Conrad" as his pen name in 1895, his passport read "Korzeniowski" until 1921. See Zdzisław Najder's excellent biography, *Joseph Conrad: A Chronicle* (New Brunswick, N.J.: Rutgers University Press, 1984), 10, for his conclusions regarding Conrad's birthplace.

2. Frederick R. Karl, *Joseph Conrad: The Three Lives* (New York: Farrar, Straus and Giroux, 1979), 225. Conrad called *Moby-Dick* "a rather strained rhapsody with whaling for a subject and not a single sincere line in the 3 vols of it." Quoted in *The Collected Letters of Joseph Conrad, volume 3, 1903–1907*, eds. Frederick R. Karl and Laurence Davies (Cambridge: Cambridge University Press, 1988), 408. The Dostoyevsky comment was included in a letter printed in Edward Garnett, ed., *Letters from Joseph Conrad: 1895–1924* (Indianapolis: Bobbs-Merrill, 1928), 260–61. See also *Letters, volume 4, 1908–1911*, eds. Karl and Davies, 526, footnote 4.

3. *Letters, volume 2, 1898–1902*, eds. Karl and Davies, 35.

4. Three letters to Spiridion Kliszczewski, in *Letters, volume 1, 1861–1897*, eds. Karl and Davies, 12–14.

5. Paul Langlois, quoted in Najder, 110.

6. Joseph Conrad, *Last Essays* (London: J. M. Dent & Sons, Ltd., 1926), 25. This essay, written in November 1923, was the last substantial piece Conrad completed, according to Najder, 483.

7. Galsworthy was one of several acquaintances to win the Nobel Prize for literature, an award that eluded Conrad to the end.

8. For *Almayer's Folly* Conrad wrote a preface, his earliest

critical statement. It was rejected by Unwin and not printed until 1920 when it was included with the author's notes that Conrad wrote for the collected edition of his works.

9. *Letters*, 1:267–68.

10. Najder, 195.

11. The preface was printed with the final installment in William Ernest Henley's *New Review*, but was withheld from the book publication by Heinemann. It was restored years later in the collected edition of Conrad's works.

12. *Letters*, 2:173.

13. One other product of the collaboration with Ford was a negligible short novel, *The Nature of a Crime*. It was begun in 1906 but not published in book form until the year of Conrad's death. A preface Ford persuaded him to write in 1924 was the last completed piece written by Conrad.

14. *Letters*, 3:54.

15. James quoted in Karl, *Three Lives*, 744.

16. Conrad quoted in ibid., 746.

17. Conrad quoted in Najder, 102.

18. Conrad quoted in ibid., 432.

19. Conrad quoted in ibid., 451.

20. Forster quoted from his *Abinger Harvest* (1936), in Najder, 461.

21. In a 1920 diary entry Woolf explained the "decline" in Conrad's art: "He never sees anyone who knows good writing from bad, and then being a foreigner, talking broken English, married to a lump of a wife, he withdraws more and more into what he once did well, only piles it on higher and higher, until what can one call it but stiff melodrama." Quoted in Thomas C. Moser, *Joseph Conrad: Achievement and Decline* (Cambridge: Harvard University Press, 1957; Hamden, Conn.: Archon Books, 1966), 209.

22. A short play, *Laughing Anne*, based on his 1914 short story "Because of the Dollars," and written at the end of 1920, at least netted Conrad £100 from an eager manuscript collector, Thomas

J. Wise. Ironically, like Henry James's works in recent years, Conrad's novels have inspired a number of successful cinematic and televison productions.

23. G. Jean-Aubry, ed., *Joseph Conrad: Life and Letters*, 2 vols. (Garden City, N.Y.: Doubleday, 1927), 2:309–10.

24. Conrad quoted in Najder, 490.

Chapter 2: Awareness beyond Ability

1. Joseph Conrad, *A Personal Record* (Garden City, N.Y.: Doubleday, Page & Co., 1924), 92. My citations of Conrad's works will be based on the twenty-four volumes of the Canterbury Edition, published in 1924. This same edition, augmented by *Suspense* and *Tales of Hearsay*, was issued in 1926 as the Kent Edition.

2. Jean-Aubry, 1:13. As late as 1907 Conrad wrote to Edward Garnett: "You remember always that I am a Slav (it's your *idée fixe*) but you seem to forget that I am a Pole. You forget that we have been used to go to battle without illusions." *Letters*, 3:492.

3. *Letters*, 1:362. Helen Watson's fiancé was Edward L. Sanderson, a young friend who may have contributed something to Conrad's conception of Lord Jim's psychology.

4. *Letters*, 3:409.

5. Jean-Aubry, 2:185.

6. See, in Conrad's *Notes on Life and Letters*, Garden City, N.Y.: Doubleday, Page & Co., 1924), 17, his discussion of Henry James as "the historian of fine consciences," where he suggests that the fine conscience is aware of more good and evil and of more truth than is the coarser conscience.

7. Here Conrad anticipates William Faulkner's expressed concern with "the problems of the human heart in conflict with itself." The phrase occurs in Faulkner's Nobel Prize acceptance speech, which owes much to Conrad's ideas and rhetoric.

Chapter 3: Ethical Agents Who Are Falsely Aware

1. The Sri Lankan R. A. Goonetilleke pronounced Conrad's Malayan world to be "predominantly authentic" and credited him

with the abiliy to rise above "Western prejudices." *Developing Countries in British Fiction* (Totowa, N.J.: Rowman and Littlefield, 1977), 92.

2. Lingard, a major figure in *The Rescue* (1920), will be the subject of discussion in a later chapter.

3. Conrad's Malayan novels, and particularly the African stories "Heart of Darkness" and "An Outpost of Progress," with their treatment of the abuses of colonialism, provided inspiration for the achievement of novelists Chinua Achebe, of Nigeria, and Ngugi wa Thiong'o, of Kenya. The South African critic Ezekiel Mphahlele has praised Conrad, along with E. M. Forster and William Faulkner, for his skillful handling of cross-cultural themes.

4. This topic will be treated in some detail in chapter 11.

5. *Letters*, 1:185. At this time of writing Conrad planned for Willems to commit suicide "because of vanity."

Chapter 4: Ethical Agents Who Are Unaware

1. The phrase occurs in *The Nigger of the "Narcissus,"* and in fact served as the title of the novel's first American edition, presumably because of the publisher's reluctance to include an opprobrious word on the book's cover. Embarrassment over this, as in the case of Mark Twain's use of the term in *The Adventures of Huckleberry Finn,* persists today. It is fair to say that neither Conrad nor Mark Twain intended the kind of insulting implication that has come to reside in the word.

2. In chapter 4, for example, Conrad resumes omniscience and enters the mind first of the chief mate and then of James Wait. Other lapses distort the focus of the book a bit, but these slips occasion no real harm to the conception of the story.

3. *Letters*, 1:423. Ian Watt, in his *Conrad in the Nineteenth Century* (Berkeley: University of California Press, 1979), 350–51, observes that this view of consciousness, a "frequent burden of Conrad's letters," is echoed by the philosopher Miguel de Unamuno in his *The Tragic Sense of Life* (1923): "Man, by the very fact of . . . possessing consciousness, is . . . a diseased animal. Consciousness is a disease."

4. Robert F. Haugh, for example, in *Joseph Conrad: Discovery*

in Design (Norman: University of Oklahoma Press, 1957), 18, concludes his interpretation of *The Nigger of the "Narcissus,"* by asserting that "there is no cosmic nihilism in Conrad's view of the Universe."

5. I do not find convincing Jakob Lothe's argument, in his stimulating study *Conrad's Narrative Method* (Oxford: Clarendon Press, 1989), 114–16. Lothe believes that MacWhirr emerges "a wiser and more imaginative human being at the end of the novella."

6. For example, Jukes receives his instructions from MacWhirr while his head is held "in chancery" by the captain.

Chapter 5: Tragic Awareness—Marlow

1. Stein, one of Conrad's most celebrated figures, to be treated later, will exhibit a psychology surprisingly close to that of Singleton and MacWhirr.

2. Albert Guerard, *Conrad the Novelist* (Cambridge: Harvard University Press, 1958), 126.

3. In this respect he is to be compared with Tom Lingard, whose name is applied to more than one persona, as he migrates from the early Malay novels to the very late final version of *The Rescue*.

4. Jocelyn Baines, *Joseph Conrad: A Critical Biography* (New York: McGraw-Hill, 1960), 202–3.

5. Skillfully promoted by Doubleday's young assistant A. A. Knopf, *Chance* became a near best seller on both sides of the Atlantic.

6. Moser, 39. Conrad's art, I feel, is aimed at demonstrating that these fragments of truth can never be assimilated into a whole.

7. Guerard, 126.

8. Unaccountably, Steve Ressler, in his fine study of *Joseph Conrad: Consciousness and Integrity* (New York: New York University Press, 1988), 71, asserts that "Brierly committed suicide at the *possibility* that he might dishonor himself [Ressler's emphasis]." Marlow's reappraisal of the man clearly hints that Brierly had made an unsuccessful effort to repress guilt for some disgrace from which he had "run away." This is mirrored, I feel, in Conrad's subtle

presentation of the French lieutenant's apparent success in suppressing *his* secret flaw.

9. This "flattering view" should be compared with the doubling of attitudes held by Jim and Gentleman Brown at the end of their lives.

10. Conrad here is halfway between Coleridge's Ancient Mariner and Albert Camus' Jean-Baptiste Clamence, in *The Fall.*

11. Jakob Lothe, who regards the French lieutenant episode as "arguably the most successful in the whole novel" (*Narrative Method,* 158–59), calls him an "utterly dependable and severely factual" officer. He also cites Jacques Berthoud, *Joseph Conrad: The Major Phase* (London: Oxford University Press, 1978), and R. A. Gekoski, *Conrad: The Moral World of the Novelist* (London: Elek Books, 1978), as both deeming the lieutenant to be Jim's antithesis by virtue of his moral integrity. Lothe himself senses that the moral position of Conrad is more ambiguous and more complex than that of the lieutenant.

12. See, for example, Robert Penn Warren's introduction to the Modern Library edition of *Nostromo* (1951), xxii, where he declares Stein's speech about the "destructive element" to be the central passage in *Lord Jim.* Warren's essay was reprinted in R. W. Stallman, ed., *The Art of Joseph Conrad: A Critical Symposium* (East Lansing: Michigan State University Press, 1960; Athens: Encore Edition, Ohio University Press, 1982), 218.

13. Frederick R. Karl, *A Reader's Guide to Joseph Conrad* (New York: Noonday Press, 1960; modest revision issued in 1969 by Farrar, Straus, & Giroux), 127. Conrad's satiric view of any human presumption to being a providence has already been noted in his earliest novels.

14. Guerard, 142.

15. The priest image, applied to Stein as well as to the French lieutenant, lends some credence to Royal Roussel's intelligent speculation that, after all, Stein may have been guilty of wrongdoing in spite of—because of!?—Marlow's protestation: "It is impossible to suspect Stein." See his *The Metaphysics of Darkness.* (Baltimore: Johns Hopkins Press, 1971), 93.

16. Marlow refers to his own "familiar devil" in his very first speech in *Lord Jim.* John Lester has a detailed discussion of Con-

rad's "use of the demonic and its natural prey, the soul," in his *Conrad and Religion* (New York: St. Martin's Press, 1988), 87. The book also contains a useful chapter dealing with Conrad's biblical allusions and other religious imagery.

17. Marlow's connection with this character reflects an actual relationship Conrad was cultivating in 1890, prior to his own journey to Africa. Marguerite Poradowska was the wife of a distant cousin of Conrad. An established writer herself, and a resident of Brussels, she used her influence to secure for Conrad his appointment as captain of a river steamer on the Congo River. Conrad maintained a correspondence with his "Aunt" Marguerite for twenty years. See Karl, *Three Lives,* especially 276–82; and Najder, 118–22.

18. T. S. Eliot's debt to Conrad is signaled by an epigraph sometimes printed with his poem "The Hollow Men." Ironically, Ezra Pound persuaded Eliot to remove from *The Waste Land* a projected epigraph from "Heart of Darkness."

Chapter 6: Tragic Awareness–Mrs. Gould

1. Written in Richard Curle's copy of the novel, according to Jocelyn Baines, *Critical Biography,* 301. Readers today can read this work as remarkably prescient of the political complications in Central and South America in the late twentieth century.

2. In a letter to Ernst Bendz in 1923. See Jean-Aubry, 2:296. Lothe, 177, impressed with the exceptional importance of setting in *Nostromo,* argues that "the protagonist proper is the town of Sulaco"!

3. Curiously, Stephen K. Land, in his *Conrad and the Paradox of Plot* (New York: Macmillan, 1984), identifies not one but "four focal figures" in the novel, no one of which is Emily Gould. Land's discussion "Four Views of the Hero," is reprinted in Harold B. Bloom, ed., *Joseph Conrad's "Nostromo"* (New York: Chelsea House, 1987), 81–102.

4. Nostromo is a blend of the Italian words for "our man." Ironically, his surname suggests reliability, faithfulness to an engagement.

5. For Sanford Pinsker who, curiously, sees *Nostromo* as a

"comedy of language" rather than a tragedy, Mrs. Gould is "Costaguana's Madonna incarnate," ultimately reduced by the Gould Concession to "maternal abstraction." *The Languages of Joseph Conrad* (Amsterdam: Editions Rodopi N.V., 1978), 70, 72.

6. Compare Marlowe's lie to Kurtz's fiancée.

Chapter 7: The Secret Agent

1. Daniel R. Schwarz, *Conrad: "Almayer's Folly" to "Under Western Eyes"* (Ithaca: Cornell University Press, 1980), 157.

2. See Avrom Fleishman, *Conrad's Politics: Community and Anarchy in the Fiction of Joseph Conrad* (Baltimore: Johns Hopkins Press, 1967), especially the chapter on "The Symbolic World of the Secret Agent." Also helpful is Eloise Knapp Hay's chapter on this novel in *The Political Novels of Joseph Conrad: A Critical Study* (Chicago: University of Chicago Press, 1963). See also John A. Palmer's discussion of "Anarchists and Revolutionaries" in his *Joseph Conrad's Fiction: A Study in Literary Growth* (Ithaca: Cornell Univerity Press, 1968).

3. The innocent Stevie falls between two other Christ figures: Dostoyevsky's idiot, Prince Myshkin, and Benjy, of Faulkner's *The Sound and the Fury*.

4. Anthony Winner comments at length on the metropolitan milieu of *The Secret Agent:* "The frequent foulness of London approximates in a sleezy, secondhand way the horrors of the Congo. . . . The authorial distaste is aesthetic as well as moral." *Culture and Irony: Studies in Joseph Conrad's Major Novels* (Charlottesville: University Press of Virginia, 1988), 70–72.

Chapter 8: Under Western Eyes

1. Avrom Fleishman, in *Conrad's Politics,* 219, has shown that Conrad's treatment of the assassination of Mr. de P——— is actually a conflation of details taken from accounts of the assassination of Czar Alexander II in 1881 and the assassination in 1904 of the interior minister, V. K. De Plehve.

2. The phrase "one of us," so meaningful in *Lord Jim,* has occurred in this novel more than once already. But notice especially

here Conrad's ironic use of Marlow's favorite designation as employed by one of the conspirators.

3. In the light of Conrad's heated rhetoric here, it is interesting to note that he wrote John Galsworthy of an early plan to have Razumov marry Natalia, with his confession and "the death of these people . . . brought about mainly by the resemblance of their child to the late Haldin." See *Letters*, 4: 9.

4. See Fleishman, 219–20, for an account of the historical basis for the incident in which Mikulin discloses to Peter Ivanovitch the duplicity of Nikita when they meet by chance on a train traveling in Germany. According to Fleishman, the head of Ochrana, A. A. Lopuchin, betrayed the police spy Evno Azoff to the revolutionary leader Vladimir Burtsev. Lopuchin, like Mikulin, eventually fell from grace and was demoted and exiled. Incidentally, Conrad's treatment of the "heroic fugitive," Peter Ivanovitch, is closely patterned on the experience of the anarchist Bakunin, who escaped from Siberia in 1861 and made his way to England.

Chapter 9: "The Secret Sharer"

1. Like so many of Conrad's tales, "The Secret Sharer" is based on a germ of fact. An officer of the clipper *Cutty Sark* who killed a crewman in a fight was allowed by the captain to "escape." The captain, possibly a model for Brierly in *Lord Jim*, committed suicide shortly thereafter. See Norman Sherry, *Conrad's Eastern World* (Cambridge, England: Cambridge University Press, 1966), 253–69.

Chapter 10: Victory

1. The language teacher, in *Under Western Eyes*, admits to Natalia Haldin that he has done little else but "look on."

2. This unnamed narrator even echoes Marlow's language: "Morrison was 'one of us.' " He evinces the same leisurely loquacity and delivers his opinions with, at times, the same coy irony. The narrator does not, however, descend to the self-conscious preciosity of the Marlow of *Chance*, which predated *Victory* by a couple of years.

Chapter 11: Lingard the Rescuer

1. The fictional figure named Tom Lingard appears to have been rather closely patterned on an actual William Lingard, of a prosperous English trading family in the Dutch East Indies, who was known to Conrad, at least by reputation, as an enterprising sea captain and trader whose adventurous activities earned him the title of Rajah Laut, "King of the Sea." See Karl, *Three Lives*, 242–49, for an account of this source.

According to Avrom Fleishman, the prototype for the fictional Lingard in *The Rescue* was Sir James Brooke, a "free-enterprise imperialist" who arrived as a seaman-trader in Sarawak on the island of Borneo in 1839, eventually displaced the local ruler, set himself up as Rajah, and ruled his kingdom "independently of—even in opposition to—the mother country" (*Conrad's Politics*, 99).

Rajah Brooke, whose mythical exploits certainly attracted Conrad's admiration, was also a source for the Patusan phase of Lord Jim's career. See Fleishman's chapter "Colonists and Conquerors" for an able treatment of the complex political background of Conrad's Malayan fiction. Helpful background material is also to be found in Eloise Knapp Hay's study of the political novels, as well as in the early work of John Dozier Gordan, *Joseph Conrad: The Making of a Novelist* (Cambridge: Harvard University Press, 1940; Russell & Russell, 1963).

2. Cf. Stein's disastrous "remedy" for Lord Jim.

3. This is the germ of the plot of *The Rescue*.

4. Vernon Young, in his "Lingard's Folly: The Lost Subject," judged this section to contain "the weakest writing" in the book. (The essay, which first appeared in *Kenyon Review* in 1953, is reprinted in Stallman's *Critical Symposium*, 96–108.) But I agree with Paul Wiley, who praised Conrad's success here in conveying "through an elaborate impression of cosmic disturbance a parodied version of divine judgment." See his *Conrad's Measure of Man* (New York: Gordian Press, 1966; reprint of the book published in 1954 by the University of Wisconsin Press), 43.

5. The book has not been without its admirers, including André Gide. Karl, in *Three Lives*, 860, quotes extensively from a letter in which Gide told Conrad that he found in *The Rescue* the same *"noblesse désespérée, la même détresse morale,"* that he had found in his favorite Conrad novel, *Lord Jim*. Karl then comments: "Read-

ing *The Rescue* through Gide's eyes, we are forced to see, despite its flaws of characterization and language, a greater weight than is usually granted; we notice a certain grandness to Conrad's scheme, from Gide's reading."

Camille R. La Bossière is among those who recently have praised the artistic merit of this book. See his *Joseph Conrad and the Science of Unknowing* (Fredericton, New Brunswick: York Press, 1979), 65–66. Daniel R. Schwarz discusses "the significance and continuity of *The Rescue*" in his *Conrad: The Later Fiction* (London: Macmillan Press, 1982), 105–24. Robert Caserio acclaims Conrad's "Romance of the Shallows" as a fine demonstration of "representational algebra." See his article *"The Rescue* and the Ring of Meaning," in *Conrad Revisited: Essays for the Eighties,* edited by Ross C. Murfin (University, Ala.: University of Alabama Press, 1985).

6. Conrad himself pointed to such differences between the early and late manuscripts of the book. See Jean-Aubry, 2:209.

7. Gordan, 28. Surprisingly, Paul Wiley, 175, reduced Lingard's story to "the history of his degeneration."

8. Vernon Young, in Stallman, 96.

9. Nearer, that is, in his 1947 monograph published by New Directions. In 1958 (in *Conrad the Novelist,* 71) Guerard appeared to accept Young's reverse ordering of the novels and, by this "historical reordering and abstraction," to derive from "three fairly separate novels" what he called "the pessimistic burden of Conrad's Malayan trilogy."

10. Frederick Karl actually used the term to describe the novel's "soft, unsure, even meretricious" center. See Karl's *A Reader's Guide to Joseph Conrad,* 281. Moser (63–64) based his judgment on a letter written by Conrad to his publisher, and quoted in part by Jean-Aubry (1:164, note 1). The whole citation in Jean-Aubry reads as follows: "If the virtues of Lingard please most of the critics, they shall have more of them. The theme of it shall be the rescue of a yacht from some Malay vagabonds and there will be a gentleman and a lady cut out according to the regulation pattern." A reader familiar with Conrad ought to detect the irony in these words. There is apparently no sure way to determine precisely when Conrad thought of "introducing" the yacht people into "The Rescuer"; but I have already shown that a yacht rescue was in Conrad's mind as early as 1895, and in fact was credited in *An Outcast of the Islands* (14) to the prowess of Lingard.

Incidentally, this rescue episode has occasioned other surprises in interpretation. Daniel Schwarz, for example (in *Conrad: The Later Ficton*, 111–12), believes that when Lingard saves the yacht, "he mimes Conrad's fantasy that he will rescue Polish civilization"!

11. Moser, 68. On the other hand, Royal Roussel, in his *The Metaphysics of Darkness* (Baltimore: Johns Hopkins Press, 1971), 71, has argued that the writing of *The Rescue* from the beginning threatened Conrad with an experience of "the darkness." For Roussel, the completion of the book after more than twenty years "marks not only the destruction of Conrad's belief in the integrity of man and his world, but the dissolution of his commitment to an art which is the expression of this belief."

12. Moser, 146.

13. An example written by a psychiatrist is Bernard C. Meyer's *Joseph Conrad: A Psychoanalytic Biography* (Princeton University Press, 1967). The book has all the interest and limitations of this kind of approach to literary criticism. Zdzisław Najder has provided a sane and balanced critique of the persisting notion that Conrad viewed heterosexual love as the "uncongenial subject." See Najder, 362–64.

14. Meyer suggested that Lingard's virility is sustained by an almost fetishistic love for his brig, *Lightning*. His involvement with Mrs. Travers only "exposed his impotence," and Edith Travers herself, incredibly, is a "frigid heroine." (230, 341)

15. Karl, in his *Reader's Guide to Joseph Conrad*, 283–84, equated Willems's infatuation with Aïssa and Lingard's passion for Edith Travers—and added, "the theme of the novel is Lingard's loss of manhood in the face of sensual infatuation."

16. I cite Moser so constantly because the influence of his brilliant analysis persists in Conrad scholarship.

17. Moser, 146.

18. Ibid., 147.

19. The shift in Conrad's approach to the "providence" theme may be detected in two scenes in *The Rescue*. Once talking to Edith Travers, after overhearing crewmen discuss the desperate situation, Lingard with self-directed irony echoes their sentiment: "I am, under Providence, to serve your turn."

And the faithful Jaffir, who Conrad says "had acquired the habit of pious turns of speech in the frequentation of professedly religious men," intones: "Our refuge is with Allah." Conrad adds that actually Jaffir "reposed all his trust in Lingard who had with him the prestige of a providential man sent at the hour of need by heaven itself." All of this is a long way from the parodic material in *An Outcast of the Islands*.

20. Moser, 148.

21. Ibid., 151–52.

22. D'Alcacer's persuasive power with Mrs. Travers mirrors Martin Decoud's Mephistophelian influence on Mrs. Gould in *Nostromo*.

23. *Letters*, 1:381. There are those who are inclined to distrust everything that Conrad (or any other writer) says about his own work. Easy targets of their skepticism, of course, are the author's notes, most of which Conrad composed near the end of his career for the collected edition of his works. Presumably they are factual, insofar as his memory served him, but they can be misleading. Certainly more dependable are the comments he addressed to publishers and to intimate literary associates like Edward Garnett and R. B. Cunninghame Graham.

24. Hay, 96–97.

Chapter 12: Ordeal by Decision: "A Choice of Nightmares"

1. *Letters*, 1:424–25.

2. Ibid., 2:16–17.

3. Ibid., 2:24.

4. Ibid., 2:25.

5. Ibid., 2:60 and 68.

6. Ibid., 2:64.

7. Ibid., 2:90. Here Conrad comes close to making explicit the theme I have been tracing in his fictional art. Earlier (January 31, 1898) Conrad had written Cunninghame Graham (2:30): "If we

could only get rid of consciousness. What makes mankind tragic is not that they are the victims of nature, it is that they are conscious of it. To be part of the animal kingdom under the conditions of this earth is very well—but as soon as you know of your slavery the pain, the anger, the strife—the tragedy begins. . . . Our refuge is in stupidity, in drunken[n]ess of all kinds, in lies, in beliefs, in murder, thieving, reforming—in negation, in contempt—each man according to the promptings of his particular devil." Twenty years later he wrote John Quinn: "That is the tragedy—the inner anguish—the bitterness of lost lives, of unsettled consciences and of spiritual perplexities. Courage, endurance, enthusiasm, the hardest idealism itself, have their limits. And beyond those limits what is there? The eternal ignorance of mankind, the fateful darkness in which only vague forms can be seen which themselves may be no more than illusions." See Karl, *Three Lives*, 807–8.

8. *Letters*, 2:131.

9. Ibid., 2:136.

10. Ibid., 3:64. Wells, at the end of his life, in 1945, with most of his hopes blasted by mankind's reverses in two world wars, succumbed to a mood as intensely despairing as any Conrad ever knew.

11. Ibid., 4: 116. But Conrad earlier (Nov. 11, 1901) had cautioned Galsworthy: "The fact is you want more scepticism at the very foundation of your work. Scepticism the tonic of minds, the tonic of life, the agent of truth—the way of art and salvation." Ibid., 2:359.

12. Karl Jaspers, *Man in the Modern Age*, translated by Eden and Cedar Paul (Garden City: Doubleday Anchor, 1957), 210.

13. *Letters*, 2:159. Conrad added in the next paragraph: "La société est essentielment criminelle—ou elle n'existerait pas."

14. Carter, in *The Rescue*, before responsibility matured him—or did it?—was of a nature that is "helped by a cheerful contempt for the intricate and endless suggestions of thought."

15. The last, presumably, in a Jungian, racial sense.

16. Somewhere in Conrad is the observation that a man always takes credit for his good luck.

17. At the outset I acknowledged the futility of attempting to

impose any typology on the rich variety of Conrad's creations. My categories of awareness have, I hope, been useful in their suggestiveness. Readers can apply them or modify them as they see fit. For example, in *The Secret Agent*, a heavily ironic novel, Verloc, the Professor, Inspector Heat, the Assistant Commissioner, Stevie, and Ossipon comprise a parade of characters manifesting many kinds and degrees of false awareness. The reader has seen that Winnie Verloc had only an "instinctive" comprehension that things do not stand much looking into.

In *Under Western Eyes*, Haldin, the political revolutionary, appears to have been guided in his judgments and actions by an idealist's false awareness; and Razumov, so much like the creations of Dostoyevsky whom Conrad professed to despise, was driven in his criminal action and in his confession by impulses that obscured a genuinely tragic awareness such as that which darkly illuminated the ordeals of Mrs. Gould, Lingard, and Marlow.

Victory, in many ways a disappointing book, presents a deluded Lena who in her dying enjoys an ironically empty victory. And Axel Heyst, who was damned both by action and by the avoidance of action, who halfway through the novel declared that "he who forms a tie is lost," is hardly convincing in his final deposition ("Ah, Davidson, woe to the man whose heart has not learned while young to hope, to love—and to put its trust in life") and in his melodramatic demise.

18. In *Lord Jim*, it will be remembered, Marlow observed that some desperate encounters require "an enchanted and poisoned shaft dipped in a lie too subtle to be found on earth."

19. Cf. Archibald MacLeish, in *J.B.* (Boston: Houghton Mifflin Co., 1958), 22. The Satan-figure tells Zuss (God):

"I know what hell is now—to *see*.
Consciousness of consciousness. . . ." [MacLeish's emphasis]

A Select Bibliography

Works by Joseph Conrad

(Listed in order of earliest publication)

Almayer's Folly, 1895.

An Outcast of the Islands, 1896.

The Nigger of the "Narcissus" (published in the United States as *Children of the Sea: A Tale of the Forecastle)*, 1897.

Tales of Unrest (containing "Karain: A Memory," "The Idiots," "An Outpost of Progress," "The Return," and "The Lagoon"), 1898.

Lord Jim: A Tale (also titled *Lord Jim: A Romance)*, 1900.

The Inheritors: An Extravagant Story (written in collaboration with Ford Madox Ford), 1901.

Youth: A Narrative and Two Other Stories (containing also "Heart of Darkness" and "The End of the Tether"), 1902.

Typhoon, 1902.

Typhoon and Other Stories (containing also "Amy Foster," "To-Morrow," and "Falk"), 1903.

Romance: A Novel (with Ford Madox Ford), 1903.

Nostromo: A Tale of the Seaboard, 1904.

The Mirror of the Sea: Memories and Impressions, 1906.

The Secret Agent: A Simple Tale, 1907.

A Set of Six (containing "Gaspar Ruiz," "The Informer," "The Brute," "An Anarchist," "The Duel," and "Il Conde"), 1908.

Under Western Eyes: A Novel, 1911.

A Personal Record (first called *Some Reminiscences)*, 1912.

'Twixt Land and Sea (containing "A Smile of Fortune," "The Secret Sharer," and "Freya of the Seven Isles"), 1912.

Chance: A Tale in Two Parts, 1913.

One Day More: A Play in One Act (based on "To-Morrow"), 1913.
Victory: An Island Tale, 1915.
Within the Tides: Tales (containing "The Planter of Malata," "The Partner," "The Inn of the Two Witches," and "Because of the Dollars"), 1915.
The Shadow-Line: A Confession, 1917.
The Arrow of Gold: A Story between Two Notes, 1919.
The Rescue: A Romance of the Shallows, 1920.
Notes on Life and Letters, 1921.
The Secret Agent: Drama in Four Acts (based on the novel), 1921.
The Rover, 1923.
Laughing Anne: A Play (based on "Because of the Dollars"), 1923.
The Nature of a Crime (with Ford Madox Ford in 1908), 1924.
Suspense: A Napoleonic Novel (left unfinished), 1925.
Tales of Hearsay (containing "The Warrior's Soul," "Prince Roman," "The Tale," and "The Black Mate"; preface by R. B. Cunninghame Graham), 1925.
Last Essays (edited by Richard Curle), 1926.
Congo Diary and Other Uncollected Pieces (including "The Sisters," a fragment dating from 1895–96; edited by Zdzisław Najder), 1978.

Conrad's Correspondence

Jean-Aubry, G., ed. *Joseph Conrad: Life and Letters*, 2 vols. Garden City, N.Y.: Doubleday, 1927. The initial is variously stated to stand for Georges or Gérard. G. Jean-Aubry was the form the editor's name took in this publication. His later book on Conrad, *The Sea Dreamer* (translated by Helen Sebba, 1957), was published as by Gérard Jean-Aubry. The Library of Congress identifies the name as Georges. The author's name is sometimes listed as Aubry, Georges Jean.

Curle, Richard, ed. *Conrad to a Friend: 150 Selected Letters from Joseph Conrad to Richard Curle*. New York: Crosby, Gaige, 1928.

Garnett, Edward, ed. *Letters from Joseph Conrad, 1895–1924* Indianapolis: Bobbs-Merrill, 1928.

Gee, John A., and Paul J. Sturm, eds. *Letters of Joseph Conrad to Marguerite Poradowska, 1890–1920*. New Haven: Yale University Press, 1940.

Blackburn, William, ed. *Joseph Conrad: Letters to William Black-wood and David S. Meldrim.* Durham, N.C.: Duke University Press, 1958.

Najder, Zdzisław, ed. *Conrad's Polish Background: Letters to and from Polish Friends.* London: Oxford University Press, 1964.

Randall, Dale B. J., ed. *Joseph Conrad and Warrington Dawson: The Record of a Friendship.* Durham, N.C.: Duke University Press, 1968.

Watts, C. T., ed. *Joseph Conrad's Letters to Cunninghame Graham.* Cambridge, England: Cambridge University Press, 1969.

Karl, Frederick R., and Laurence Davies, eds. *The Collected Letters of Joseph Conrad.* Volume 1: *1861–1897* (1983). Volume 2: *1898–1902* (1986). Volume 3: *1903–1907* (1988). Volume 4: *1908–1911* (1990). These first four volumes published by Cambridge University Press. Four additional volumes are projected.

Works about Joseph Conrad

Baines, Jocelyn. *Joseph Conrad: A Critical Biography.* New York: McGraw-Hill, 1960.

Berthoud, Jacques. *Conrad: The Major Phase.* Cambridge, England: Cambridge University Press, 1978.

Bloom, Harold, ed. *Joseph Conrad's "Nostromo."* New York: Chelsea House, 1987.

Bonney, William W. *Thorns & Arabesques: Contexts for Conrad's Fiction.* Baltimore: Johns Hopkins University Press, 1980.

Bradbrook, Muriel C. *Joseph Conrad: Poland's English Genius.* Cambridge, England: Cambridge University Press, 1941. Reissued by Russell and Russell, 1966.

Conradiana: A Journal of Joseph Conrad Studies. Lubbock, Texas: Texas Tech University, 1968 to present. Three issues per year.

Cooper, Christopher. *Conrad and the Human Dilemma.* London: Chatto & Windus, 1970.

Cox, C. B. *Joseph Conrad: The Modern Imagination.* London: J. M. Dent, 1974.

Ehrsam, Theodore G. *A Bibliography of Joseph Conrad.* Metuchen, N.J.: Scarecrow Press, 1969.

Fleishman, Avrom. *Conrad's Politics: Community and Anarchy in the Fiction of Joseph Conrad.* Baltimore: Johns Hopkins Press, 1967.

Fogel, Aaron. *Coercion to Speak: Conrad's Poetics of Dialogue.* Cambridge, Mass.: Harvard University Press, 1985.

Gekoski, R. A. *Conrad: The Moral World of the Novelist*. London: Elek Books, 1978.

Gillon, Adam. *The Eternal Solitary*. New York: Bookman Associates, 1960.

Goonetilleke, D. C. R. A. *Developing Countries in British Fiction*. Totowa, N.J.: Rowman and Littlefield, 1977.

Gordan, John Dozier. *Joseph Conrad: The Making of a Novelist*. Cambridge, Mass.: Harvard University Press, 1940; Russell & Russell, 1963.

Graver, Lawrence. *Conrad's Short Fiction*. Berkeley: University of California Press, 1969.

Guerard, Albert J., Jr. *Conrad the Novelist*. Cambridge, Mass.: Harvard University Press, 1958.

———. *Joseph Conrad*. New York: New Directions, 1947.

Haugh, Robert F. *Joseph Conrad: Discovery in Design*. Norman: University of Oklahoma Press, 1957.

Hay, Eloise Knapp. *The Political Novels of Joseph Conrad*. Chicago: University of Chicago Press, 1963.

Hewitt, Douglas J. *Conrad: A Reassessment*. Cambridge, England: Bowes and Bowes, 1952; 2nd ed., 1969.

Johnson, Bruce. *Conrad's Models of Mind*. Minneapolis: University of Minnesota, 1971.

Karl, Frederick R. *Joseph Conrad: The Three Lives*. New York: Farrar, Straus and Giroux, 1979.

———. *A Reader's Guide to Joseph Conrad*. New York: Noonday Press, 1960; revised 1969.

Kirschner, Paul. *Conrad: The Psychologist as Artist*. Edinburgh: Oliver & Boyd, 1968.

La Bossière, Camille R. *Joseph Conrad and the Science of Unknowing*. Fredericton, New Brunswick: York Press, 1979.

Leavis, F. R. *The Great Tradition*. London: Chatto and Windus, 1948.

Lester, John. *Conrad and Religion*. New York: St. Martin's Press, 1988.

Lohf, Kenneth A., and Eugene P. Sheehy. *Joseph Conrad at Mid-Century: Editions and Studies, 1895–1955*. Minneapolis: University of Minnesota Press, 1957.

Lothe, Jakob. *Conrad's Narrative Method*. Oxford: Clarendon Press, 1989.

Meyer, Bernard. *Joseph Conrad: A Psychoanalytic Biography*. Princeton: Princeton University Press, 1967.

Morf, Gustav. *The Polish Heritage of Joseph Conrad.* London: Sampson, Low, Marston, 1930.

——. *The Polish Shades and Ghosts of Joseph Conrad.* New York: Astra Books, 1976.

Moser, Thomas C. *Joseph Conrad: Achievement and Decline.* Cambridge, Mass.: Harvard University Press, 1957, Hamden, Conn.: Archon Books, 1966.

Murfin, Ross C., ed. *Conrad Revisited: Essays for the Eighties.* University, Ala.: University of Alabama Press, 1985.

Najder, Zdzisław, ed. *Conrad under Familial Eyes.* Translated by Halina Carroll-Najder. Cambridge, England: Cambridge University Press, 1983.

——. *Joseph Conrad: A Chronicle.* Translated by Halina Carroll-Najder. New Brunswick, N.J.: Rutgers University Press, 1983.

Palmer, John A. *Joseph Conrad's Fiction: A Study in Literary Growth.* Ithaca, N.Y.: Cornell University Press, 1968.

Pinsker, Sanford. *The Languages of Joseph Conrad.* Amsterdam: Editions Rodopi N.V., 1978.

Ressler, Steve. *Joseph Conrad: Consciousness and Integrity.* New York: New York University Press, 1988.

Rosenfield, Claire. *Paradise of Snakes: An Archetypal Analysis of Conrad's Political Novels.* Chicago: University of Chicago Press, 1967.

Roussel, Royal. *The Metaphysics of Darkness: A Study in the Unity and Development of Conrad's Fiction.* Baltimore: Johns Hopkins Press, 1971.

Said, Edward. *Joseph Conrad and the Fiction of Autobiography.* Cambridge, Mass.: Harvard University Press, 1966.

Schwarz, Daniel R. *Conrad: "Almayer's Folly" to "Under Western Eyes."* Ithaca, N.Y.: Cornell University Press, 1980.

——. *Conrad: The Later Fiction.* London: Macmillan Press, 1982.

Sherry, Norman. *Conrad: The Critical Heritage.* London: Routledge and Kegan Paul, 1973.

——. *Conrad's Eastern World.* Cambridge, England: Cambridge University Press, 1966.

——. *Conrad's Western World.* Cambridge, England: Cambridge University Press, 1971.

Stallman, R. W., ed. *The Art of Joseph Conrad: A Symposium.* East Lansing: Michigan State University Press, 1960; Encore Edition by Ohio State Press, 1982.

Teets, Bruce E., and Helmut E. Gerber. *Joseph Conrad: An Annotated Bibliography of Writing about Him, 1895–1966.* DeKalb, Illinois: Northern Illinois University Press, 1971.

Tennant, Roger. *Joseph Conrad.* New York: Atheneum, 1981.

Thorburn, David. *Conrad's Romanticism.* New Haven: Yale University Press, 1974.

Watt, Ian. *Conrad in the Nineteenth Century.* London: Chatto and Windus, 1980.

Wiley, Paul L. *Conrad's Measure of Man.* Madison: University of Wisconsin Press, 1954; Gordian Press, 1966.

Winner, Anthony. *Culture and Irony: Studies in Joseph Conrad's Major Novels.* Charlottesville: University Press of Virginia, 1988.

Wright, Walter F. *Romance and Tragedy in Joseph Conrad.* Lincoln: University of Nebraska Press, 1949.

Yelton, Donald C. *Mimesis and Metaphor: An Inquiry into the Genesis and Scope of Conrad's Symbolic Imagery.* The Hague: Mouton, 1967.

Zabel, Morton Dauwen. "Joseph Conrad: Chance and Recognition," *Sewanee Review* 53 (Winter 1945): 1–22. Zabel also wrote the introduction to the first edition of the Viking *Portable Conrad* in 1947.

Index